Praise for *Hell and Its Problems*

"We have rarely met with a clearer and more reasonable exposition of the generally accepted doctrine of Hell and kindred subjects.... The writer certainly makes clear one point, whatever may be said of others, and that is the necessity of recognizing Hell as an essential element in the whole Christian scheme and the consequent lack of consistency on the part of those who think themselves justified in rejecting the one whilst accepting the other.... The style is equal to the matter—clear, smooth, trenchant."

—*Truth*

"The author is no fossil—in theology or in science. It is what we have to believe about Hell, we, the heirs of the ages, that he tells us. There seems no escape from his logic or appeal."

—*Expository Times*

"A little book capable of doing immense good.... It is a model of the manner in which the unchanging doctrine concerning Hell and eternal punishment ought to be presented to the modern mind."

—*Universe*

"This is one of Mr. Raupert's best books—the clearest and fullest exposition of the doctrines of Hell in our language."

—*Ave Maria*

"We gladly note the appearance of these thoughtful studies on one of the most widely misunderstood of Christian dogmas. They are orthodox in doctrine and are excellently reasoned out, and they will no doubt do a great deal of good in dispelling the popular and mostly shallow objections commonly urged against the Catholic teaching on this most important subject. The whole book is thoughtful and stimulating; we give it a cordial welcome."

—*Tablet*

"The author's study is a very model of what is required. It is well written, concise, forcible, scientific without being technical, happy in its quotations and perfectly adapted for popular use. The author goes straight to the very kernel of the subject."

–*Catholic Book Notes*

"The author is a thinker and knows how to make an advantageous use of his wide and intelligent reading relevant to the subject under consideration."

–*Christian Age*

"The book deserves a wide welcome.... It is singularly free from all exaggeration and is a model of exposition."

–*Catholic Times*

"As a philosophical and logical treatment of a difficult subject, it would be hard to improve on Mr. Raupert's exposition."

–*Catholic Herald*

"The most popular arguments against Hell are met and answered in a masterly manner.... This volume is bound to do good."

–*Monitor*

Hell and Its Problems

Also by J. Godfrey Raupert
from Sophia Institute Press:

Christ and the Powers of Darkness

J. Godfrey Raupert, K.S.G.

HELL
and Its
PROBLEMS

SOPHIA INSTITUTE PRESS
Manchester, New Hampshire

Previously published in 1917 by Catholic Union Store, Buffalo, New York. This edition by Sophia Institute Press contains minor editorial revisions and deletions to the original text, so that the book will be applicable to a wider audience.

Cover design by Updatefordesign Studio.

Unless otherwise noted, Scripture references in this book are taken from the King James Version.

Nihil obstat: H. B. Laudenbach, *Censor Librorum*
Imprimatur: D. J. Dougherty, Bishop of Buffalo
Buffalo, New York, November 8, 1917

Nihil obstat: Eduardus Myers, *Censor Deputatus*
Imprimatur: Edm. Can. Surmont, *Vicarius Generalis*
Westmonasterii, June 7, 1912

The *nihil obstat* and *imprimatur* are official declarations that a book or pamphlet is free of doctrinal or moral error. No implication is contained therein that those who have granted the *nihil obstat* and *imprimatur* agree with the contents, opinions, or statements expressed.

Sophia Institute Press
Box 5284, Manchester, NH 03108
1-800-888-9344
www.SophiaInstitute.com

paperback ISBN 979-8-88911-088-0

ebook ISBN 979-8-88911-089-7

Library of Congress Control Number: 2023945168

First printing

Contents

Preface

The publication of this little treatise is prompted by several considerations. Experience and observation have convinced me that the orthodox doctrine of Hell presents to many serious and thoughtful minds one of the greatest stumbling blocks in the way of a wholehearted and intelligent acceptance of the truths of the Christian Creed. I am equally convinced that, in view of the immovable foundation upon which the doctrine rests, the compromise offered by modern liberal theology—and, indeed, all attempts to explain the doctrine away—are but calculated to increase the intellectual and moral difficulty a thousandfold.

To very many persons, the better philosophical and theological works fairly and adequately dealing with the subject are either unknown or are, by reason of their technical form, and for other obvious reasons, of little service.

Comparatively few are acquainted with the unexpected disclosures of modern psychical science and the light that these are calculated to throw upon the mysteries enveloping the future life. They are, therefore, scarcely in a position to think the matter out clearly and dispassionately and to weigh the considerations that can, in fairness, be urged in favor of the truth of the doctrine, from the human point of view.

Having personally experienced the full force of the moral difficulty that belief in the orthodox doctrine of Hell involves, and having given a good deal of study and time to the matter, I felt that a short statement of the views arrived at, and of what really careful thinkers have written on the subject, might prove suggestive and helpful to other perplexed and troubled minds.

The subject obviously is one that does not readily lend itself to popular treatment, and the ideas expressed are therefore necessarily somewhat crude and fragmentary in their form and character. They may, nevertheless, induce some who, for one reason or another, have rejected the doctrine—and, as is so often the case, other fundamental doctrines with it—to study the subject with greater care, and to reconsider their conclusions. They will, at any rate, help them to see that there are better and more solid grounds for believing the doctrine than is commonly supposed.

The first issue of this volume was published under a pseudonym some years ago at the suggestion of a learned theologian. In its present form, it has undergone but slight alterations, a few thoughts only having been modified and several further considerations and quotations added.

1

The Christian Doctrine of Hell

It is admitted by all really fair and unbiased minds that the orthodox doctrine of Hell is a vital and necessary part of the Christian revelation. The scriptural and historical evidence in its favor is so exceptionally clear and conclusive that there can be no reasonable ground for doubt or choice in the matter. Nor is there any legitimate way of effecting an honorable compromise with modern rationalistic thought and interpretation. The doctrine is not only taught by Christ Himself in the plainest and most unmistakable terms of which human language is capable, but it underlies and is implied in the entire system of thought developed in the New Testament and may be said to be its very basis and foundation. Without the conception of a future and permanent state of punishment consequent upon a life of sin and rebellion against God, the Christian scheme of redemption has neither consistency nor coherence, and its most central doctrines become unreasonable and incomprehensible.

This fact is, and should be, clear to all honest students of this great subject whose judgment has not been perverted by sophistical reasoning and who are determined to be loyal to fact and to truth. For it does not really matter whether the subject be studied in the original Greek of the New Testament or in one of the more modern English versions of the Bible; whether allowance be made for the language of illustration and metaphor or for the most recent discoveries of the higher critic. It is not a question of particular words or phrases or expressions but of great ideas and principles—of an element that is intimately bound up with the entire thought structure of the Sacred Writings and pervades and permeates its every part.

It is instructive and significant to observe that this transparent fact has never been questioned by the skeptic and the unbeliever, however strongly he may have opposed the doctrine itself on moral grounds. "It has been reserved for the accommodating, shallow Christians of modern days who wish to reject it without abandoning their belief in Christianity, to throw dust in other people's eyes, as well as their own, by obscuring what is really a very simple matter with ingenious—though it may be unconscious—sophistries."

But it may be doubted whether any permanent service has thus been rendered to the cause of Christianity and of truth. Such literary tricks may impress the superficial few; they have little, if any, weight with really logical and consistent thinkers. Their worthlessness is bound to be detected sooner or later. For it is impossible, by any method or artifice, to get rid of the plain and striking statements of Holy Writ. Such words as are employed by Christ Himself in Matthew 25:41, 46, in Mark 3:29 and 9:47–48, and in Revelation 14:10–11 and 21:8 remain, as the late Sir James Stephen rightly said, "the most terrific words which have ever been spoken in the ears of man"; and they will retain their force and import, however ingenious the attempt may be to empty them of their meaning. In such a matter as this, it is surely a dangerous thing for the mind to seek refuge in a false security and to allow to take root the impression that, by ignoring the unwelcome truth, it has ceased to exist for us or that we have escaped the responsibilities that its recognition entails. Our duty is rather to face it bravely and, God helping us, to seek for safe and legitimate and God-appointed means of escape.

It is assumed by very many intelligent persons that the orthodox conception of Hell is inconsistent with reason and with cultivated thought and that it has been rejected by a large number of really thoughtful theologians. Loose statements to this effect are frequently made from Protestant pulpits, and they are apt to impress the modern mind seriously. But a greater error cannot be conceived. The most cultured and enlightened among Catholic and Protestant theologians, of both ancient and modern times, have explicitly stated it as their most earnest conviction that the doctrine is a vital and integral part of the New Testament teaching and that the only safe and honest thing is to acknowledge the fact.

St. Augustine, one of the greatest and most learned Fathers of the Christian Church, says:

> What a thing it is to account eternal punishment to be a fire of long duration (merely), and eternal life to be without end, since Christ comprised both, in that very same place, in one and the same sentence, saying: "These shall go into eternal punishment, but the just into life everlasting." If both are eternal, either both must be understood to be lasting with an end, or both perpetual without end. For like is related to like: on the one side, eternal punishment, on the other, eternal life. But to say in one and the same sentence life eternal shall be without end, punishment eternal and Hell have an end, were too absurd; whence, since the eternal life of the saints shall be without end, punishment, eternal too, shall doubtless have no end to those whose it shall be.[1]

1 *De Civitate Dei,* 21, 23.

Carlo Passaglia, S.J., a renowned theologian and a man well qualified to speak with authority on this subject, well observed: "Either St. John and Isaiah used terms expressive of eternal duration, or else there is no such term to be found."

"Every form of words employed in Scripture to describe everlastingness," wrote Dr. Angus, "our Lord and His Apostles employ to describe the state of those who die in sin and disbelief."[2] Or, as Mr. Oxenham, a Roman Catholic writer, expresses it: "The most uncompromising revelation of this awful truth, which no rationalizing sophistry can effectually obscure, issued from the lips of the Incarnate Word Himself."

Such are the views of some really careful and learned thinkers on this great subject who, we may suppose, were fully alive to the moral difficulties that their conclusions involved. Numerous others might be quoted were it not that this volume is to be of limited size and is not to assume the form of a theological treatise. But if this be so, what are we to say of those modern pseudo-theologians who, to please the spirit of the age, attack the very central stronghold of the Faith, even at the risk of discrediting Christianity itself and of loosening its hold upon the human mind? There is, as has been rightly said, nothing so contemptible as skepticism masquerading in a surplice. There is nothing so offensive and grotesque as the picture of the modern critic apologizing for his belief and accommodating its central verities to the rationalizing tendencies of the age in which he lives. It is a very striking instance of the salt losing its savor, of the blind leading the blind—of revealed truth, instead of restraining and modifying human thought and action, humbly adapting itself to the supposed claims of human reason.

[2] Joseph Angus, *Future Punishment: An Inquiry into Scripture Teaching* (London: Hodder and Stoughton, 1871), 11.

And it must be clear that the moral perils involved in such an attitude of mind are of exceptional magnitude and that they are of necessity far-reaching in their influence upon conduct and character. Fear of punishment, it is true, is not the best and highest motive for right-doing; but it is a very powerful motive nevertheless and, with certain orders of mind, the only influence that is active in restraining and controlling the moral life.

"The Passion and Hell," wrote the late Father F. W. Faber, "are the two great foundations out of which men learn a profound hatred of sin; they are the two wellheads of sacred fear; they are two revelations of God most necessary to complete a true idea of Him."[3]

The truth of these assertions may be called in question by some modern philosophers who speak of man as he exists in their own imagination and who have formulated a Christianity after their own hearts; they will not be denied by those who have stood face-to-face with the great problems of social and moral evil and who know from practical experience what man really is.

Any such authoritative denial of the doctrine of Hell, moreover, is bound to be disastrous to earnest faith in the central verities of the Christian religion. In the Christian scheme of redemption, one doctrine depends on the other, one implies and explains the other, and the bond that unites them cannot be severed without loosening each separate link and without rendering the whole scheme illogical and unreasonable. The doctrine of Hell is a necessary part of this scheme, and a denial of it is almost always followed by denial of some other important doctrine connected with the Incarnation and Redemption of Christ. It inevitably leads to what are termed "advanced" and "liberal" views, and what is this but another name for disbelief, or rejection, of truths that the natural

[3] Frederick William Faber, "Heaven and Hell," in *Spiritual Conferences*.

human reason cannot square with its dictates and surmises and against which the unaided intellect rebels?

The religious movements of the present day, and the normal attitude of numbers of intelligent persons toward the historic Faith are surely striking evidence in support of this statement. To hold orthodox views—in other words, to believe what God has manifestly revealed even though the mind may not be able to grasp it fully, has come to be regarded as a sign of imperfect education, or of inferior intellect, and there are scores of people who would think it nothing short of a personal insult were one to regard them as still believing in the existence of the orthodox Hell.

Some of them, of course, have never been taught to think logically and accurately, and they merely echo the predominating views of the multitude. Some have no clear notion of what the doctrine of Hell really teaches, and they direct their attack not so much against the doctrine itself as against some popular and unwarrantable exposition of it. Some have been carried away by the postulates of their natural reason and by a supposed conflict between the ascertained facts of modern science and revealed religion. The greater number, by far, are the victims of half-instructed and skeptical religious teachers who lack the courage necessary for withstanding the stream of modern tendencies and who are perhaps vaguely conscious that they would be of but small reputation did they not advance with that stream. But the result is the same in either case. It is doubt and distrust of the essential truths of revelation and an attitude of mind that amounts to a practical rejection of them.

The disappearance of Hell, by a logical process of thought and inference, transforms the entire conception of the nature of sin and its consequences. A modified and more "rational" notion of sin invalidates the doctrine of the Atonement and Redemption, and the readjustment of that doctrine again throws doubt upon the nature and divinity of Christ. Thus, step by step, the subtle work of destruction goes on, and it is completed only when the supernatural element of Christianity has disappeared and the disclosures of Christ respecting human duty and human destiny have either been explained away or have been adapted to the claims of unilluminated human reason.

It is sometimes assumed—and, in many instances, even boldly asserted—that science, so far as it can be expected to express an opinion on such a subject, of necessity pronounces against the doctrine of Hell and that the latter stands in violent antagonism to the ascertained laws of nature and of life. But this impression, too, has no foundation whatever in fact. On the contrary, the modern doctrine of the conservation and correlation of forces testifies in favor of the existence of Hell and, granting another life, indeed almost postulates it as a physical necessity. There are eminent scientific men who, reasoning from the reign of ascertained law in the physical universe, have inferred the reign of unchanging law in the spiritual universe and have thus found reasonable grounds, on scientific principles, for defending and maintaining the Christian doctrine of Hell.

Some years ago, an eminent biologist gave expression to his views on this point in the following words:

> Now, any being to whom has been given that wonderful power will, with all the consequent responsibilities of a state of probation, must be able to fail as well as to succeed—the very term "probation" implies a risk of failure. What are we to deem probable as to the consequences of such failure? Reason unaided can tell us very little of the soul after death. Certainly we have no evidence that it will then be

able to undo what it has done during life, but rather the contrary. The doctrine of the persistence of force does not favor such a view, and there is nothing that contradicts the Church's assertion that the state in which the soul finds itself at the close of life's trial cannot be reversed. If so, the man who dies in a state of aversion from the highest light and the supreme good must remain in such a state with all its inevitable consequences.

Some will say those consequences need not be eternal. But if the cause should be unchangeable, how can the consequences change? Moreover, we are contemplating what relates to eternity, when time shall have ceased to be.[4]

The learned authors of that deeply interesting work *The Unseen Universe* wrote as follows:

> To some extent, no doubt, Christ's description of the universal Gehenna must be regarded as figurative, but yet we do not think that the sayings of Christ, with regard to the unseen world, ought to be looked upon as nothing more than pure figures of speech. We feel sure that the principle of continuity cries out against such an interpretation—may they not rather be descriptions of what takes place in the unseen universe, brought home to our minds by means of perfectly true comparisons with the processes and things of this present universe which they most resemble? Thus the Christian Gehenna bears to the unseen universe precisely the same relation as the Gehenna of the Jews did to the city of Jerusalem. And just as the fire was always kept up, and

[4] St. George Mivart, "Happiness in Hell," *Nineteenth Century* 32 (July–December 1892): 908–909.

> the worm ever active in the one, so are we forced to contemplate an enduring process in the other. For we cannot easily agree with those who would limit the existence of evil to the present world. We know now that the matter of the whole of the visible universe is of a piece with that which we recognize here, and the beings of other worlds must be subject to accidental occurrences from their relation with the outer universe in the same way as we are. But if there be accident, must there not be pain and death? Now, these are naturally associated in our minds with the presence of moral evil. We are thus drawn, if not absolutely forced, to surmise that the dark thread known as evil is one which is very deeply woven into that garment of God which is called the universe. In fine, just as the arguments of this chapter lead us to regard the whole universe as eternal, so in like manner are we led to regard evil as eternal, and therefore we cannot easily imagine the universe without its Gehenna, where the worm dieth not and the fire is not quenched. The *process* at all events would seem to be most probably an enduring one.[5]

In a striking work on *The Natural History of Hell*, an American writer says:

> Every phenomenon is the result of preceding causes, and becomes itself the cause of other occurrences, and this obtains both in the moral and physical world.... If the consequences of every act cling to us for all time, then the consequence of our wrong-doing can be no

[5] Balfour Stewart and P. G. Tait, *The Unseen Universe, or Physical Speculations on a Future State* (New York: Macmillan, 1875), no. 254.

exception. The wrong-doer will go down through all the endless cycles of eternity chained to his doom, not by the arbitrary sentence of a capricious judge, but by the adamantine links of cause and effect, working in strict accord with laws whose action knows no pity and no mitigation. Compared with such links the iron chains which bound the vulture-gnawed Prometheus to his rock are but as cords of silk and ropes of sand. From such a doom there is no escape but by a miracle....

That the intellect and moral sensibilities may be rendered more delicate and more acute is within the range of our knowledge and experience. Some men seem to be under the influence of a moral anaesthetic, and do not feel the keen pain which results from knowing that they have done ill. But let the moral sense be awakened, and an increased knowledge attained of the evil results of their actions, and then the intellectual torture becomes fearful.

As is well known to medical men, cases often arise in which the nervous system becomes supersensitive, and the prick of a pin, or the slightest touch gives exquisite pain. Let us imagine that, after a career of crime, the moral and intellectual sensibilities of the evil-doer should be rendered intensely acute, can we imagine a more terrible Hell than that to which he would thus be consigned?

If these sufferings are the normal result of natural laws, then, so long as these laws maintain their sway, there is no escape, and can be no pardon. Pardon—that is release from misery—can only come by a suspension of these laws, or, in other words, by a miracle.

Thus far, then, science leads us and no farther. When she has pronounced our doom she shows no way of pardon

> or escape; and he who relies upon natural laws and the general beneficence of the Creator, must see that in this there is no promise of mitigation. If left to Nature, and to Nature's laws, we can only sit down in the dust and cry, "Woe is me!"[6]

The testimony of many other thoughtful minds might be adduced in order to demonstrate the fact that disbelief of the orthodox doctrine of Hell is not, as is sometimes supposed, the characteristic of really deep and searching thinkers but, on the contrary, an evidence of superficial reflection and of hasty generalization. The pride of the half educated, as one has well said, always discovers a shortcut to unbelief.

In the course of an elaborate discussion of a kindred subject *The Spectator* not very long ago remarked:

> It certainly cannot be shown that either progressive purification or progressive degradation necessarily comes to an end . . . nor have we the smallest vestige of evidence that the downward progress of the will is a terminable process, and comes to any natural end. It may do so if immortality depends only on the union with God. But there is certainly a sort of antagonism to God, which appears to be progressive, as well as the union with Him, and antagonism means conscious existence no less than love means conscious existence. All we can say is that if a man be what Mr. Gladstone terms *immortalisable*, there is no final reason (unless it be God's mercy) why he should not be immortalisable in one direction as well as in the other; and that, while a

[6] John Philipson, *The Natural History of Hell* (New York: Industrial Publication Company, 1894), 98–102.

> good deal of our moral and spiritual experience tends to show the durability of remorse, and the persistence of the growing incapacity to turn back after a certain point in the downward stage is reached, we have only the vaguest hope to rely on for our anticipation that all suffering must finally end.[7]

"This, at least, is true," says another learned writer on the subject, "that we can find in the study of observed spiritual and moral phenomena, and in the comparison of indisputable laws of God's creation, an indication, such as prompts the watcher of the skies to expect the appearance of a new planet, that an eternal doom of evil must be awaiting sin just beyond the grave."[8]

Again, the doctrine of Hell is declared to be in conflict with the testimony of our normal moral instincts. This is perhaps the most popular objection of all and is one that is supposed to settle the matter finally. But this objection, too, has no foundation in fact. There is such a thing, of course, as an artificial conscience, a way of silencing the natural voice of the soul by sophistry and reasoning. Our moral nature can, with a certain kind of manipulation, be made to witness falsely. But the *unperverted* instinct of man, his normal, natural conscience, unquestionably testifies in favor of some grievous punishment consequent upon sin and final impenitence.

Africa

The ancient Egyptians taught and believed that the souls of the sinful must appear before the judgment seat of Osiris to be condemned to successive incarnations in the bodies of animals.

7 "Is Man Immortal?," *Spectator* (August 24, 1895): 235.

8 "Everlasting Punishment," *Dublin Review* 5 (January–April 1881): 127.

A similar belief is held by the Libyans, the Ethiopians, and the various races of modern Africa. The wicked souls pass into the hands of the wicked spirit in his dark habitation or wander about in the air or in the forest, full of malice and restlessness.

Asia

As regards the Asiatic races, the ancient Persians taught that the souls of the godless pass into the power of the evil spirit.

According to the belief of the Indians, the soul appears before the judge of the dead immediately upon leaving its body. The soul of the wicked goes to Hell, there to be tormented in various ways. The ancient Chinese teach that the souls of the wicked join the company of evil spirits or wander about in various forms in graveyards and other places. The Japanese, too, exclude all sinful souls from Heaven.

America and South Sea Islands

The Greenlanders believed that the souls of the wicked are condemned to a deep subterranean region that is without warmth and light and where they are full of fear and terror.

The Mexicans held that the wicked go to the lower regions, where various places exist for various crimes.

According to the belief of the Peruvians, the souls of wicked men are banished to a place in the center of the earth where there is no rest, but sickness and trouble of various kinds.

Native Americans, too, had a conception of Hell, where the wicked must eat bitter fruits or are cast into a deep well in which fire is burning.

Many of the South Sea Islanders believed that the wicked go to a dark country where the sun never shines and where there is only muddy water.

Europe

The Hell of the old Germanic races was a deep precipice where the old envious serpent had her being and was incessantly gnawing at the roots of the tree of life, in perpetual enmity with the spirit of God. Those races believed that in this Hell murderers and perjurers were tortured forever.

The proper place of punishment of the old Greeks and Romans was Tartarus. We know from classic sources what the nature of its terrors was. Similar to what we read in Virgil and Ovid are the expressions used by the Greek poets Homer, Pindar, Euripides, Sophocles, and Aristophanes and by philosophers such as Pythagoras, Socrates, Aristotle, and Plato.

By the latter we have that famous sentence (*Phaedo*):

> Those whose condition, by reason of the heinousness of their crimes, are seen to be incurable, a well-deserved fate hurls into Tartarus, which they never leave again.

In this unanimous testimony of both cultivated and uncultivated races and nations, we have the universal instinctive convictions of mankind expressed. And it seems to me that whatever allowance we may have to make with respect to the particular *form* in which this belief expresses itself, it is impossible to assume that, in the matter of the belief itself, all these races and nations should have been allowed to fall into error.

But this "voice of nature" clearly is not in agreement with the voice of "enlightened" modern reason!

On the other hand, we have to recognize the fact that, by far, the larger majority of mankind are restrained from evil action and from self-indulgence not by the love of God and of good but by the fear of punishment, vaguely felt by the conscience to be certain and inevitable. It is this motive alone that rules and regulates the wills and affections of those whose normal tendencies are altogether downward and who cannot be said to be restrained by any secondary law governing the social life. They may not be able to define the mysterious power that is thus working in their moral nature; they may even be inclined to deny its existence; but it is there, nevertheless, and is apt at certain times to make itself most practically and unpleasantly felt.

The false liberalism of the age has given rise to the notion that the fear of punishment is one of the lower and unworthier motives that lead men to do right and to pursue and cultivate high and spiritual ideals rather than ignoble and earthly ones. And human vanity has readily adopted this notion as a kind of truism—demonstrating, as it is supposed to do, that we have left childish and savage things behind us and have reached a more exalted stage in our moral evolution. But it seems to me that a subtle self-deception lies behind this popular notion. A superficial study even of human life and human character constantly exhibits its fallacy. It is most certainly not love of God that restrains even refined and cultivated men from an indulgence of their passions and from entering upon crooked and forbidden paths in the various relationships of life. What does restrain them is the sense and fear of punishment—in the form of dishonor and loss of social prestige in the temporal order and of dimly discerned, perhaps, but nevertheless conceivably serious consequences in the spiritual order.

The recognition of this fact may be humiliating to our pride and self-conceit, but its importance will be recognized by all those who take the matter seriously and who are determined to see things as they really are.

And, admitting this fact, what is the revealed doctrine of Hell but a confirmation of these vague instincts and promptings of nature—the warning voice of God speaking here and now in emphatic and unmistakable terms.

"Menace as well as promise," wrote Mr. Gladstone,

> menace for those whom promise could not melt or move, formed an essential part of the provision for working out the redemption of the world....
>
> So far as my knowledge and experience go, we are in danger of losing this subject out of sight and out of mind. I am not now speaking of everlasting punishments in particular, but of all and any punishment intelligibly enforced; and can it be right, can it be warrantable that the pulpit and the press should advisedly fall short of the standard established by the Holy Scriptures, and not less uniformly by the earliest and most artless period of hortatory Christian teaching? Is it not altogether undeniable that these authorities did so handle the subject of this penal element, in the frequency of mention and in the manner of handling, that in their Christian system it had a place as truly operative, as clear, palpable, and impressive, as the more attractive doctrines of redeeming love? I sometimes fear that we have lived into a period of intimidation in this great matter. That broad and simple promulgation of the new scheme which is known as the Sermon on the Mount was closed with the awful presentation of the house built upon the sand.[9]

With these wise words, based on an accurate knowledge of the Scriptures, and, of course, on the many-sided experiences of a life

[9] Right Hon. W. E. Gladstone, *Studies Subsidiary to the Works of Bishop Butler* (Oxford: Clarendon Press, 1896), 199, 206.

affording unique opportunities of insight into human character, I most thoroughly agree.

It cannot be accidental, surely, that Holy Scripture contains far more warnings of Hell than promises of Heaven. He who searches "the hearts and reins" knows what truth is best calculated to stay and direct the weak and frail mind of man (see Ps. 7:10[9]). I feel confident that when the secret history of each saved soul comes hereafter to be revealed, it will be found that the fear of Hell has saved more souls from Hell than the promises of Heaven. Although fear is not the highest motive to virtue, it is the most common one nevertheless—and, in the critical moment of life, the most powerful one beyond doubt.

But from whatever point of view we may be disposed to regard the matter, it is certain beyond all possible doubt that the doctrine of Hell—of eternal punishment—is both explicitly and implicitly taught by Christ and by the Apostles, and by all the saints and martyrs, and the really great theologians after their time and that it is one of the very cornerstones upon which the Christian system of redemption and restoration reposes. And, admitting this fact, it is surely an unpardonable offense on the part of some modern teachers, often for the sake of notoriety, to waver and hesitate in fully declaring this truth or so to veil and obscure it as to empty it of its full moral weight and import. In the face of the momentous interests at stake, such a mode of action is not charity but cruelty and unfaithfulness.

> If indeed so terrible a doom awaits the finally impenitent, the surest guarantee for escaping it hereafter is not to forget it now. If the doctrine of eternal punishment be a revealed verity it is treason to God and treachery to men to withhold or disguise it, or tamper with it, because we may choose to

> think it better to leave them in ignorance of what He has taught it better to reveal.
>
> To presume upon overriding the express declarations of the Lord Himself, delivered upon His own authority, is surely to break up Revealed Religion in its very groundwork, and to substitute for it a flimsy speculation, spun, like the spider's web, by the private spirit, and about as little capable as that web of bearing the strain by which the false is to be severed from the true.[10]

One fact most certainly remains: the doctrine of Hell may be rejected—its truth cannot be disproved, and the disquieting thought remains that it is conceivable. It may well be that the difficulty does not lie in the doctrine itself but in the limitation of the natural intellect, which cannot reason conclusively respecting the things of the supernatural order.

But, if the doctrine be true, unbelief will be seen to be a far more perilous thing than at first sight appears. The denial may in itself seem trivial; but, by the consequences of it, we may forfeit the means of attaining salvation, since we thus put ourselves outside the reach of Christ's method of redemption. Those, therefore, who deny it should have a very high degree of instinctive certainty, or they are guilty of fearful levity. A man intending to commit suicide may change his mind when he is in the water, but he may, for all that, be unable to catch hold of the rope that is held out to him, and he may perish. The consequences would be the same as in the case of the man who will not catch hold of the rope. Rightly, therefore, does Diderot say: "A sensible man will act in

[10] Right Hon. W. E. Gladstone, "Speculations on the Future of the Unrighteous," *Public Opinion* 20 (January–June 1896): 529.

life as though there was a Hell so long as a fragment of doubt as to the existence of Hell remains in his mind." And the Christian Church, if she is to fulfill her mission and the central aim of her institution, has no alternative but to proclaim the truth as her Divine Founder committed it to her. Her duty is to control human thought and speculation, not to be controlled and influenced by them. She cannot modify any one of her doctrines, "or tamper with the exactness of its expression even though by doing so she would win half the world. Her mission is to convert the nations to the truth, not to adapt the truth to them, and every attempt to do so must be fatal alike to the cause of truth and to the souls it is designed to serve."[11]

It should be borne in mind that our inability to understand the doctrine of Hell fully, or to reconcile it with our imperfect and limited conception of justice and of right, cannot possibly constitute an argument against its truth. We might with equally good reason reject every other doctrine of the Christian religion. The most important and central of them escape full intellectual apprehension. We see at best but as "through a glass, darkly" (1 Cor. 13:12). Indeed, we would expect that beings like ourselves, whose nature is limited and is under the "false seemings" of the senses, would have but an imperfect apprehension of the truths of divine revelation. There would always be the difficulty of expressing divine and eternal things in human and changeable, and consequently inadequate, terms.

> Let it be observed … that we are not bound to be able to solve all difficulties which may be urged against a thesis which from other sources is abundantly proved. Even in

[11] Rev. H. G. S. Bowden's preface to *Revealed Religion*, by F. Hettinger.

matters of physical science no one expects this. There are difficulties against the law of gravitation itself which cannot be solved, yet no one thinks of doubting the existence of the law. Revelation has its difficulties, but so has existence itself. Revelation has its mysteries, but so has rationalism. Meanwhile, the certainties which we rightly hold must be held devoutly, and the difficulties may well wait their fuller solution in the light of a brighter day.[12]

[12] "Everlasting Punishment," 139.

2

Some Popular Objections and Difficulties Considered

1. The Goodness of God

We are constantly told in the present day that the sins and failures of our moral life are chiefly due to our education and our social environment. There is, it is said, strictly speaking, no such thing as deliberate sin. Transgression of the moral law is not so much an act of rebellion against God as a fault of temperament and an innate lack of that strength of character that is known to exercise control over the desires and tendencies of our lower nature. And God is too good to punish man for what is, after all, due only to his natural and inherited weakness. In the progressive development of the race, the higher side of our nature is slowly but steadily being evolved, and when it shall have attained its fuller development and conquered human weakness and ignorance, sin and vice, too, and the miseries that flow from them will disappear from the earth.

This is the fashionable modern philosophy of life that, as most of us know, is professed by vast numbers of intelligent and cultivated persons. It is attractive because of its seeming reasonableness, and it has the advantage that it solves some of the most difficult problems that have ever perplexed the human mind. It certainly disposes, in the simplest and most "natural" way possible, of the claims of the Christian religion and abolishes its unattractive and seemingly unreasonable creed.

This philosophy has one serious disadvantage, however. It is emphatically contradicted by all we know of God and of His mode of action within the natural sphere of life. We certainly have no evidence whatever that, because of His goodness, He makes allowance for our innate tendencies or for the weaknesses and frailties of our nature. On the contrary, we know the very opposite to be the case. We know for certain that He is quite capable of hurting us severely, and even permanently, and that He rigidly and unerringly punishes sin.

In the natural sphere, disobedience to the laws of the physical life is invariably followed by bodily suffering and pain. Indulgence in forbidden joys and pleasures brings with it consequences that may be of the most far-reaching character. They may effectually hinder and paralyze a useful career or embitter each single joy of a long life.

In the same way, transgressions of the moral law are followed by remorse, by mental sufferings that are infinitely greater sometimes than those endured by the body. There is, we are told, nothing so terrible as the torture of an evil conscience, even though it may be possible to hide such an experience beneath a calm external demeanor. Murderers have been known to deliver themselves up to justice, after years of moral agony, solely to escape the tortures of a conscience stricken with remorse. We all admit that, by reason of our moral frailty, the pains and sorrows of our life are greater, by far, than its pleasures and joys.

From the standpoint of our imperfect knowledge, such suffering may seem severe and out of proportion to the character of the offense. We say that the transgression or the fault was due to our ignorance or perhaps to our peculiar temperament; the transgressor was scarcely responsible. But there must surely be another side to the matter, since the self-evident fact remains that, in spite of His goodness, and in spite of our ignorance and our temperament, God certainly does punish. Our personal responsibility must, as a matter of fact, be infinitely greater than we commonly suppose. Our moral intuitions certainly would seem to support this view. Conscience, in its normal manifestations, incessantly and emphatically witnesses to our responsibility. In language and promptings that we may not be able to define and analyze but that are nevertheless audible to the inner ear, conscience never ceases to remind us that, whatever our temperament, moral transgression is an act of the will and that, in spite of certain natural tendencies, we are absolutely free, and may, if we will, resist the evil and do the good. And reason itself surely points to the trustworthiness of this innate faculty since it is impossible to account for its origin except by assuming the existence of a higher moral order with which it is in correspondence.

In any case, although we cannot always reconcile God's goodness with His ways of punishment, we do not, on that account, doubt His goodness or deny the fact of His punishment. We admit both, however great the problem may be that they present, because for both there is abundant and satisfactory evidence. We constantly confess that God is good even though He punishes severely in the sphere of the natural life.

Now, if we can, in a measure, reconcile God's goodness with His severity here and now, why should we not be able, with fuller knowledge and enlarged faculties, to do so hereafter? Our difficulty may be entirely due to our ignorance and to our imperfect, and therefore mistaken, conception of things. "It is possible," says a modern writer,

> that could we understand what eternity really is, the notion of the reversal of the soul's condition might be seen

> to involve an absurdity. Moreover, such a change does not appear to us reconcilable with justice, for any temporal retribution however prolonged, would, if succeeded by eternal happiness, place all men practically on a level. For centuries upon centuries vanish into nothingness when compared with eternity. Science, at least, lends no support to the belief that a change can take place in the consequences of any action once performed. It is not inexorable severity, and the continuance of chastisement, but mercy and forgiveness which the aspects of Nature and their scientific study render difficult of belief.[13]

"Retributive justice," wrote Cardinal Newman, "is the very attribute under which God is primarily brought before us in the teaching of our natural conscience."[14]

> We know only too well that pain and agony exist here. What ground can we have for denying the possibility of their existence hereafter? Any unnecessary and useless suffering cannot, of course, co-exist with a good God. But who can pretend to know God's ultimate end in creation? That His purposes cannot contradict our clear ethical perceptions is certain, but there may be useful and benevolent ends subserved by suffering which we cannot fathom, and there may be divine purposes which, without contradicting, transcend even goodness, and which our faculties are quite unable to conceive of.[15]

[13] Mivart, "Happiness in Hell," 909.

[14] John Henry Newman, *An Essay in Aid of a Grammar of Assent*, 10, 2, 2.

[15] Mivart, "Happiness in Hell," 909.

In any case, we recognize God's goodness even though we cannot understand and fully reconcile it with His methods of punishment. We know for certain that God is not incapable of hurting us even though He is good. And if this be so here, why not there? The higher probability is that laws similar to those that we know to be in operation in the natural sphere are in operation in the supernatural sphere also.

Again, it must be borne in mind that Hell is primarily not of God's creation but of man's—no arbitrary infliction of a vengeful Deity but a law working in the inmost depths of our moral nature.

> Hell is a law. Just as it is a law that pent-up water, when its weight and force have reached a certain point, breaks its barriers and sweeps down upon the region below it, so it is a law that sin or unrighteousness or wilful aversion from God, if it reach the boundary, death, unreformed, will go on for ever so, and will bring eternal separation from God, and separation in a spiritual nature means misery.[16]

It is evident that in the world of the inner life, subtle and highly complex forces are incessantly at work. Thoughts, aims, and desires are silently but unerringly molding the character. The experiences of life, success or failure, troubles or joys, and the manner in which we accept or reject them are imperceptibly educating the heart and training the affections; self-discipline and self-control, exercised or neglected, are either strengthening or weakening the powers of the will; pure or impure desires and influences, checked or indulged in, are disposing and inclining the moral nature this way or that. The outer life, with its never-ceasing action upon the inner man, is gradually but steadily creating a distinct personality, the essential

16 "Everlasting Punishment," *Dublin Review*, 130.

characteristics of which may not be clearly known to ourselves but must necessarily be known to God.

The modern study of the subconscious man has thrown much light upon these matters and has shown how very inaccurate our judgment of the true human personality may be sometimes. We know, for instance, that the manifestly cultured and refined man who, in his outward relations to other men, is a paragon of virtue may, so far as his real inner nature is concerned, be a debased sensualist and a villainous thief and ruffian.

The best of men know how extremely difficult it is to effectually bring their inner nature into conformity with their moral convictions and the laws of the spiritual life.

Few persons probably even entertain the thought that there is the possibility of their growing morally worse and of their becoming more and more estranged from God—diverted from the pursuit of the true end of life. And yet they may be steadily degenerating, evil taking imperceptibly a firmer and more permanent hold upon them, their very lack of resistance to the downward tendencies of life sweeping them away from God.

Does not experience constantly teach us how completely the man who exclusively pursues worldly interests becomes, in the course of time, the slave of those interests? He would seem to lose the very faculty of apprehending higher and spiritual realities. The life of his soul becomes paralyzed. His heart becomes chilled. He becomes insensible to spiritual influences, to the claims of that other world that his reason all the while tells him to be the true end and aim of life. His inner light becomes dulled, his inner ear closed, so that he sometimes ends in denying the very existence of that other world. And, in a sense, it has no doubt ceased to exist for him since he stands, in the matter of his moral life, wholly outside it and apart from it. But in such a case, it is surely not God but his own weak will and his persistently misdirected aim of life that are shutting him out from the kingdom of Heaven. It is the law of sin and of death that is working the ruin and destruction of his soul. "Sow a thought," says an old adage, "and reap an action; sow an action and reap a character; sow a character and reap an eternity."

If such a man be hereafter excluded from a state of being with which he is in no sense in moral correspondence, and for the enjoyment of which he possesses no single faculty, can he in fairness call the goodness of God in question?

Again, it is urged by our opponents that love is declared to be the chief note in the gospel message. God's love for man is great. He desires his happiness. The coming of Christ, His life of suffering and humiliation, and His final sacrifice are evidence of this. How are we to reconcile the thought of Hell with such a love? Does not the latter notion of necessity exclude the former? Can we conceive of a God of love ultimately turning His back upon any man, however sinful, and of abandoning him to his fate?

It is in some such form as this that the difficulty is apt to be stated. And at first sight it seems a formidable difficulty, no doubt. A little reflection, however, shows it to be a shallow and superficial method of reasoning.

From the principles governing the actions of men in the present life, the objection stated cannot be said to receive a shadow of support. The chief or ruler of a state desires the happiness and well-being of his subjects. He puts himself and his ministers to an infinite amount of trouble to secure them. But he does not, on that account, hesitate to punish the transgressor, to deprive him, in some instances, of his liberty, and even to punish him permanently—to deprive him of life itself.

It never occurs to a single mind to question the goodness of a ruler because he condemns a man to death. The mind sees no incongruity between the first quality or characteristic and the latter action.

A good parent punishes his child and, in certain instances, even severely. There are cases on record in which an excellent father has finally abandoned and cast off a hopeless and degenerate son. The normal mind has no difficulty whatever in reconciling the two—the thought of the excellency of the father and of the casting off of the son.

Where, then, is the difficulty in God's acting in a similar fashion in His moral universe, especially when we bear in mind that His knowledge of human character and of the measure of individual responsibility is full and accurate and that His judgment cannot, in any case, be at fault?

Can we justly say that He ceases to be good because the creature He has endowed with free will persistently and determinedly misuses that will and, to the very last moment of its life, lives in open defiance of His known laws?

God's love for man is great, no doubt; but equally great, surely, must be His zeal for the moral world order—the ultimate purpose for which the universe exists. He must hate any disturbance of it, and the maintenance of this world order clearly cannot be achieved without laws guarding it and punishing offenders. But all the experience of life proves that the mere declaration of the law is useless. Men disobey it in spite of the sense of duty, the movings of conscience, social obligations, and self-respect.

By far, the larger number of thoughtful men, although they may not believe in the orthodox Hell, believe in some kind of Purgatory, in some sort of punishment for sin committed in the body. Yet how comparatively little influence has this belief upon their moral life, how few saints does it produce, how ineffectual is it in restraining them from indulging their appetites and their passions!

It is the authoritatively declared eternal consequence of the breaking of the law that braces up the will and calls the forces of the higher nature into activity.

Do we not know that looseness of morals results wherever the belief in a future life of reward and punishment has disappeared? And those who attempt to get rid of the doctrine of Hell are, for the most part, those who have also gotten rid of the idea of sin.

It is certainly a curious thing and worthy of note that to the martyrs and the saints who live very close to God, Christ's teaching respecting Hell and the punishment of sin has never presented any moral or intellectual difficulty. It has never caused them to love God less, to be less willing to die for Him, or to entertain less noble or elevating ideas of His character.

It is chiefly to the easygoing man of the world, to the child of the modern age, who often does not himself know what he really believes, that these difficulties occur. It is he who waxes eloquent as to the unreasonableness of the doctrine.

When the aged Polycarp, the disciple of St. John, was put to the torture, he said to his torturers: "You threaten me with a fire which only burns for an hour and is then extinguished. You do not know the fire of the judgment to come and of eternal punishment reserved for the wicked."

One thing we may surely regard as certain: a correct estimate of the truths of the supernatural order cannot be formed by the natural human reason, least of all by the reason that is not in some sense in rapport with God and with that other-world order.

"The natural [or sensual] man receiveth [or perceiveth] not the things of the Spirit of God (1 Cor. 2:14). They are foolishness to him. A higher light is needed in order to perceive them; that light is the gift of God, and it is by that light alone, responded to by a certain soul culture and soul development, that he can see rightly and judge justly." "Everything grows clear," said Louis Pasteur, "in the reflections from the Infinite. The more I know, the more nearly is my faith that of the Breton peasant. Could I but know all, I would have the faith of the Breton peasant woman." His intellect, in rapport with God, evidently did not urge those objections that some other intellects are urging against this and other revealed truths!

Difficulties, of course, remain and must always remain. It could not well be otherwise since we cannot see as God sees. But it is certain that the goodness of God, as exhibited in the facts of life, cannot be urged in contradiction of the doctrine of Hell. On the contrary, His present method of dealing with men is a most powerful argument in its favor. It is sentiment, not thoughtful reflection, that disputes this. "The great mystery is," as Cardinal Newman said, "not that evil should have no end, but that it had a beginning."[17]

It is surely imperfect and distorted vision, then, that only recognizes the goodness of God but pretends to see nothing of the other and severe aspects of His nature. It is folly and willful blindness to deny that they exist. "I understand not," wrote Mr. Ruskin,

> the most dangerous, because most attractive form of modern infidelity, which, pretending to exalt the beneficence of the Deity, degrades it into a reckless infinitude of mercy and blind obliteration of the work of sin: and which does this chiefly by dwelling on the manifold appearances of God's kindness on the face of creation. Such kindness is, indeed, everywhere and always visible, but not alone. Wrath and threatening are invariably mingled with the love, and in the utmost solitudes of Nature, the existence of Hell seems

[17] *Grammar of Assent*, 10, 2, 2.

to me as legibly declared by a thousand spiritual utterances as that of Heaven. It is well for us to dwell with thankfulness on the unfolding of the flower, and the falling of the dew, and the sleep of the green fields in the sunshine; but the blasted trunk, the barren rock, the moaning of the bleak winds, the roar of the black, perilous, merciless whirlpools of the mountain streams, the solemn solitudes of moors and seas, the continual fading of all beauty into darkness, and of all strength into dust—have these no language for us? We may seek to escape their teaching by reasonings touching the good which is wrought out of all evil, but it is vain sophistry. The good succeeds to the evil, as day succeeds the night, but so also the evil to the good. Gerizim and Ebal, birth and death, light and darkness, Heaven and Hell, divide the existence of man and his futurity. [Footnote: The love of God is, however, always shown by the predominance or greater sum of good in the end, but never by the annihilation of evil. The modern doubts of eternal punishment are not so much the consequence of benevolence as of feeble powers of reasoning. Every one admits that God brings good out of finite evil. Why not, therefore, infinite good out of infinite evil.][18]

2. The Justice of God

The world asks: How can a just God inflict unceasing punishment for a temporal offense, even though it be of the most heinous character? How can He punish finite sin infinitely? Punishment is a remedial measure in its ultimate aim. It is inflicted with a view

[18] John Ruskin, *The Stones of Venice*, vol. 3, chap. 3, no. 42.

to the improvement and restoration of the offender, not to his permanent suffering and misery. A convict, undergoing a long term of imprisonment for a grave offense, may obtain some alleviation and indulgence upon giving evidence of an improved moral condition. There are agencies at work for still further helping and improving him upon his restoration to the life of the world. The feeling entertained toward him is at all times that of pity and compassion. Even the death penalty is inflicted with the greatest possible reluctance and as a deterrent measure, rather than from any other motive. There are numbers of intelligent persons who, although abhorring the crime of murder, strongly condemn that penalty on moral grounds, seeing that, by it, the true end of punishment is not attained. It is, under any circumstances, felt to be an extreme and severe measure, in itself calculated to fully atone for the crime committed and, in a sense, to restore the offender to God's favor.

And is God less just and merciful than man? Is it reasonable to suppose that He will unceasingly punish for an offense for which man would punish only for a season? Might not such punishment with right be called unjust and unreasonable? Is it not cruel and vindictive?

Such is the world's familiar method of reasoning, and at first sight, we find it difficult to dispute its soundness and the common sense that apparently dictates it.

But a very brief process of reflection surely discloses the fatal flaw in the argument.

We have, in the first place, to call to mind once more that the punishment of sin is not so much God's arbitrary act as a fundamental law of the moral universe: the result of certain circumstances—a final and necessary link in the chain of cause and effect. It is the inevitable consequence of our moral freedom.

We must, in the second place, remember that it is ultimately not a question of particular acts or deeds, but of a character, of a certain definite moral state and condition, of a soul rendering itself, by its own willful and persistent attitude and action, incapable of union with God. We probably attach mistaken ideas to the words *finite* and *infinite*. We call the passing act of sin a finite act and cannot perceive how it can, under any circumstances, carry with it infinite punishment. But it is, after all, not the act of sin that brings about the punishment but the moral character that lies behind it and of which it is the outward manifestation.

The Catholic Church, moreover, teaches (and I imagine that all intelligent Protestant theologians would endorse this teaching) that it is *mortal* sin that incurs the punishment of Hell. And by *mortal sin* is not meant some act of transgression, committed through the weakness and frailty of our human nature, or even an indifferent and careless state of moral life, but sin committed *with full knowledge and consent*; or a state of life in wickedly active opposition to the known will and law of God. By *mortal sin* is understood that deliberate and willful transgression of law that is committed (1) in an important and serious matter, (2) with full and clear knowledge of the responsibility and consequences involved, and (3) with every opportunity of making an absolutely free choice.

In other words, it means an act, or an attitude of mind and will productive of or expressed in this act, that severs the bond of union existing between the Creator and the creature and that renders any reuniting of the bond impossible, since the creature is in rebellion against the Creator and has, of his own free choice, turned his back upon Him. So far, then, as a man has sinned against God, in full view of the punishment incurred, he may surely in reason be said to deserve that punishment.

But have we not a certain analogy to the divine law of punishment in our own human and imperfect modes of measuring out punishment? It is not, and cannot be, a question of time. A single act, such as a theft or a murder or a forgery, is committed in a moment of time, yet the punishment inflicted may extend over many years. The law does not determine the amount of punishment by the time occupied in committing the offense but by the nature of the offense and the moral state and character to which it points. A judge weighs all the evidence that is before him; he considers the entire life history of the offender. A single act occupying perhaps five minutes for its execution but indicating a corrupt nature may thus involve a lifelong punishment and may wreck the entire earthly career of the offender.

In the sphere of our present life, therefore, there is undoubtedly such a thing as permanent punishment for a mere temporal offense. A certain law of fitness, to which we yield instinctive obedience, seems to be at work and to lie at the root of the matter. Thus, a low moral character is universally felt to be unfit for a certain higher moral condition and environment. It has no affinity with them and is excluded from them, not always by any arbitrary act of man but by common consent.

Now, if this be so here, in this present life, where change is still possible, and where a transformation can still be effected, how is it to be there, where a terminus of life is reached, where the character is no longer capable of change, and where it is a question of a permanent moral state and condition?

In any case, it will be admitted that, in our present life, these laws are at work and that we cannot possibly escape or evade them. We do not fully understand them ourselves, and from our standpoint, they may even appear to us sometimes unfair and unjust. But it is certain that they continue in operation, nevertheless, and in spite of our views and opinions. Is it, then, unreasonable to conclude that similar fixed laws are in operation in the life beyond and that there, too, we shall not be able to evade or escape them?

Some of these laws the Christian revelation only hints at; of others, it speaks in clear and unmistakable terms. We do not like them; they appear to us unfair and unjust, and they offend our sense of the proportion of things. But they may be just laws for all that, and it is conceivable that we shall recognize them to be such when we have passed away from the life of the body and are in actual touch with the other sphere of existence. Judging from our knowledge of the present state of things, we may, at any rate, regard it as certain that they will continue in operation whether we understand them fully and approve of them or not.

Any rightly instructed Christian believes that a spiritual condition, initiated or induced by a life of moral depravity and enmity against God, must continue unless conversion and reconciliation take place. There must be a very definite and deliberate change of mind respecting God, expressing itself in confession of sin and repentance. The all-important question, therefore, is this: Is a change of mind possible after death?

Christianity says: No! Its Founder declared over and over again that forgiveness and restoration are possible only in this present life. His offer of mercy was always and distinctly limited. He never ceased urging the need of an *immediate* change of mind, since there was a time when that change would be no longer possible, and when the door of Heaven would be shut.

One would have to quote the greater part of the New Testament were one to attempt to produce scriptural confirmation of this statement.

Science says: No! Character is the ultimate and necessary result of certain moral acts and states. It is the gradual and progressive building up of a distinct organism, and it is no more possible to change the form that it finally assumes than to undo the separate acts that were instrumental in its construction.

Human experience, moreover, confirms the verdict of science. A character, it is well known, is not apt to change much after a certain age and point of evolution have been reached. It is admittedly a difficult, if not an impossible, thing to undo the subtle spiritual effect of a certain long-continued attitude of the mind.

Now, we have seen that a man remaining impenitent after an act of sin, perhaps repeating it, and thereby hastening the soul's downward course, declares enmity against God. His normal moral attitude is an attitude of opposition and rebellion. We admit that, in this state, he is unfit for the presence of God—out of touch and affinity with the sphere of the pure and the holy. But if a change be impossible after death, and death overtake him while in this state of opposition and rebellion, how is he to escape? What is to become of him? Where is he to go? He must, in that state of rebellion, appear before God. The time of probation and education is over. He is in a sphere where time is no more, where it is no longer a question of acts and attitudes of mind that can be undone and repented of but of a character, of a spiritual state that is the crown and ultimate result of all the acts and mental attitudes of many years.

Can we not here trace some faint outline of the great truth? Do not some of our difficulties melt away? Are they as great as they appear at first sight?

Even the late Dean Farrar exclaimed: "I believe that without holiness no man can see the Lord, and that no sinner can be pardoned or accepted till he has repented, and till his free will is in unison with the will of God, and I cannot tell whether some souls may not resist God for ever, and therefore may not be for ever shut out from His presence."[19]

Again, the term *eternal punishment* may be an imperfect and inadequate term: it may not nearly convey the truth as it actually is. It may be a term conveying the nearest possible equivalent to a state or condition of which we cannot, with our present limitations, form an accurate idea. Language, capable only of expressing and explaining finite things, can scarcely be expected to express the infinite adequately. May not the difficulty, therefore, be in the term rather than in the idea and principle that underlie it and that the term is meant to convey? May it not be due to the fact that our power of thought is limited and that our understandings are finite and therefore imperfect?

And it is surely untrue to maintain that the ultimate aim of all human punishment is remedial. A simple application of this theory will display its fallacy.

Let us suppose that a judge could punish only with a view to the improvement of the offender. All criminals might then be divided into two classes. Those in the first class would have no difficulty in proving to the judge their incorrigibility and hopeless moral condition; the others, their sincere regret and repentance. The aim of any kind of punishment would thus entirely disappear, and the accused would have to be discharged. But what are the facts of the case? Punishment falls again and again upon the wholly depraved in character, in whom it has never been known to produce the slightest change or improvement. A person may commit a certain offense over and over again; he may already have spent the best part of his life inside a jail, and both judge and jury may know

[19] Frederick W. Farrar, *Eternal Hope* (New York: E. P. Dutton, 1878), xxii–xxiii.

full well that no additional pain and punishment will change his character. Yet they continue to punish, simply because the social and moral order demand it. It is felt to be necessary that certain acts of sin and transgression should be met by a certain measure of suffering and punishment.

In the same way, human justice punishes the man who is already thoroughly penitent and who is not in the least likely to repeat his offense. It punishes those who, for other reasons, may be already incapable of doing further mischief. But whatever motives and ends may be assigned to such punishments, whether they be inflicted to act as a deterrent or, in some way, to bring about the improvement of society in general, it is certain that underlying them is a kind of moral necessity that all men acknowledge and to which they unhesitatingly submit.

And what is this moral necessity but an application of that law of expiation that is most certainly a marked constituent of our complex moral nature!

Sin clearly is a disturbance of the world order. It is an element entering as a disturbing agent into the harmony of the cosmos. It is fraught with injury to the individual and to society, quite apart from its supernatural aspect—its essential nature and effect from God's point of view.

And while one aim of punishment is no doubt the improvement and restoration of the offender, another and far higher aim is the restoration of the disturbed world order—expiation of the offense or sin committed. We have this fully and most clearly illustrated in the mysterious and sometimes quite incomprehensible movements of the human conscience.

Numerous instances are on record in which a criminal whose offense has remained undetected, and whose mental and moral suffering—often continued over a long period of years—may have brought him ample punishment, cannot find rest until his offense is acknowledged and his punishment is an official and public one.

It might well be urged that his mental tortures and his remorse have already improved him as well as punished him. He not only deeply regrets his sin, but he has made deliberate efforts to atone for it by a better and more careful life. He may have become a better man; yet he can find no rest. His moral nature clamors for expiation. He is satisfied only when by some public admission and pronouncement, the disturbed moral order has been restored.

But most men know that all acts of sin against God and man cause wretchedness and moral disquietude until they are expiated in one way or another. In sensitive natures, punishment is desired and even craved, although there may be no danger of the facts of the case ever becoming known. And if such punishment is secured, there is no question of any desire for moral improvement; it is a matter of expiation, pure and simple.

I cannot help feeling that a great many foolish things are said and written on this subject in our day. A simple analysis of the manifestations of one's own conscience reveals the truth about the matter. And I am convinced that there would be much more happiness in life if people recognized this truth and if, instead of craftily evading it, they obeyed the law of expiation and endured voluntary suffering for sin deliberately committed.

It is perhaps from this point of view that we come to form right ideas of some of the recorded mortifications of the saints.

Of course, this manifestation of conscience—the desire for expiation—may vary greatly in different natures. Mistaken training may lessen or almost efface it. In elevated natures, it may attain to a high degree of development. Its roots, however, are in all mankind. Hence the practice of sacrifice by all primitive as well as civilized races and nations.

Now, is it conceivable—nay, is it not highly probable?—that in the same way, a moral necessity, not clearly discerned by us in our present state but intimately bound up with the entire order of the spiritual universe, underlies the law of punishment acting in the other world? May it not be that, "could we understand what eternity really is, the notion of the reversal of the soul's condition might be seen to involve an absurdity"? At all events, it is surely a mistake to assert, in view of what has been stated, that the idea of a permanent condition of punishment violates our moral intuitions and that we have no analogy at all in our human methods of punishment? And it is surely a perilous thing to deny its possibility simply because it does not appear to fit in with the dictates of our limited and finite reason and with our human notions of justice.

But the further question has been asked: Why cannot a just and merciful God arrange His punishment in such a way as to *compel* the reformation of the offender? Why can He and does He not act upon his moral nature in such a drastic and coercive fashion as to render submission and repentance and consequent union with Himself inevitable?

This thought, however, brings us face-to-face with that greatest of all the mysteries of our human nature—our free will. It is, next to the gift of conscious life itself, the most wonderful faculty that we possess and clearly involves the gravest possible responsibility.

But, looking away from philosophic and scientific speculation and regarding the matter from the standpoint of experience, it is evident that our wills are free and that, in the moral order, God invites and impels but *never compels*. The motives for a right action or decision are put before the will, but the ultimate decision is to be man's, not God's. We are free and conscious agents, not automata.

On the other hand, admitting that God is the author of the moral law, it surely cannot be a matter of indifference to Him whether men obey it or deliberately break it.

Now, a reformation such as the above question suggests would be a compulsory reformation and therefore inconsistent with our moral freedom. But true moral improvement presupposes moral freedom and excludes compulsion. The choice, made by reason of moral coercion, would not be a free choice. It could not possibly be a test of character and of the general bent of the mind. Heaven and the enjoyment of spiritual things must ever be impossible to a nature that has been forced into them. Real moral improvement and repentance cannot be associated with the notion of compulsion.

Hence, the possibility remains of the sinner's rebelling against punishment and resisting all God's efforts with a view to his improvement and thus remaining unimproved. The possibility remains of his deliberately exercising his will in opposition to God.

Now, what is God to do with such incorrigibles? He must either continue to punish, which is eternal punishment, or He must finally receive the hopeless case into Heaven, which means the triumph of sin—rebellious man defeating God and His ultimate purpose in the moral universe. It will be seen upon reflection that no other conclusion is possible, so long as we admit the freedom of the will.

In the moral order, remedial punishment, of course, exists, but necessarily only in a temporal sense—while the soul is still swayed by conflicting motives and, consequently, still capable of change. This must of necessity cease when the character is finally fixed and when, in the case of the sinner, a definite turning away from God has taken place. The exceeding severity of some of God's temporal punishments surely involves the thought of an infinitely greater punishment to come. The latter alone rationally explains the former. For what other possible end could God be said to punish so severely? Is not the peril of permanent unhappiness an all-sufficient end?

But the secret of eternal punishment and its justice is probably fully solved only in an accurate knowledge of the real nature and effect of sin. In our present state, we can have no adequate conception as to the manner in which it affects the soul's life and shapes its destiny. We see it only in its outward manifestations, in its general effect upon character. We cannot trace its more subtle inward operations. In all probability, pride—that most terrible of all human vices—lies at the root of the whole matter. We have in the experience of life some intimation of what pride can do in the human soul. It is the source and root of almost every other evil and vice.

The terms in which sin is spoken of in the New Testament admit of no compromise and certainly lead us to infer that our conceptions of its nature and effects are most imperfect and inadequate. Christ declared sin to be the death of the soul. He pronounced no sacrifice to be too great in the effort to escape it and to overcome it. It was better, He said, that we should pluck out our eyes than that they should lead us into sin. The Apostles echoed these thoughts. The early martyrs experienced their truth and had an intense conviction of the reality of Hell and its punishments. Whenever men have grown in spiritual understanding and discernment and have, by prayer and subjugation of the lower self, cultivated the higher self, they have also changed their view as to the real nature and consequence of sin. Is it unreasonable to conclude that such a changed view is, after all, the correct one?

"Immediately after death," declares another mystic, "that natural language which lies in every man is revealed to him, and he reads at once his whole life, with its acts and omissions, in its character.

The account is engraven on his heart in figures of fire, and woe to him whose demerits weigh down the balance, who has died unrepentant in his sins, untrusting in God, and unbelieving in his Redeemer."[20]

3. Why Should Death Be Supposed to Terminate the Time of Our Probation?

Why should death be supposed to terminate the time of our probation? This is a question that has recently been asked with much seriousness and that has, in innumerable instances, received a favorable answer from the pulpit. Such an answer is probably felt to offer the only possible compromise between the clear statements of the New Testament and the claims of "enlightened" reason, and it certainly opens an acceptable way of escape out of a great difficulty. It thus becomes possible for a modern "liberal" Christian to adhere to the teaching of Holy Scripture respecting the punishment of Hell and at the same time to empty that teaching of its meaning by prolonging man's time of probation and, consequently, his chances of salvation and restoration, indefinitely.

It is but reasonable to assume, it is argued, that those endless multitudes who have never had an opportunity in this life of fully understanding and accepting the gospel message, and of whom it may safely be said that they would have accepted it had they clearly understood it, will have that opportunity given them in the life to come. Is it conceivable that these multitudes will be cast away without any such further probation? In view of the experiences of life, and of the difficulties under which men are known to labor

[20] Mrs. Crowe, *The Seeress of Prevorst: Revelations concerning the Inner Life of Man*, communicated by Justinus Kerner (New York: Patridge and Brittan, 1856), 48.

with respect to spiritual matters, does not the very thought offend our moral sense and our reason? In a thousand instances, is not life far too short to admit of anything like a completed moral education and probation? Are not thousands cut down in the very flower of their lives, when the best powers of their souls and minds are but beginning to unfold themselves and when the character may be said to be only in the process of formation?

Is it not more than probable, too, that with the increase of light shed upon the soul in the other state, a change will pass over the soul's vision and that a greater and more powerful impulse will be given to spiritual effort and endeavor? When men who have lived evil lives here on earth shall have come to see more clearly what consequences their deeds involve, are they not much more likely to repent and, thus, in the course of time, to be restored to God's favor?

The majority of us are familiar with popular questions and statements of this character. They may be said to be in everybody's mouth. They have every appearance of plausibility and reasonableness, and their acceptance certainly tends to relieve the human spirit of a weight of which it is only too conscious.

But ought we not to distrust them for that very reason? Is the human mind, in its natural state, a safe guide in matters pertaining to the supernatural order? Is man likely unaidedly to discern and accept a truth that is constantly opposing itself to his normal desires and inclinations? Is he not much more likely to make every effort to get rid of it? Reflection has shown us that he is unquestionably mistaken in the matter of his notions respecting sin, that his views in this direction are false and distorted, and that his philosophy is constructed upon his lower dictates and promptings. Is it not more than probable that, in this matter, too, he is mistaken and that, in his contention, he is but echoing his own lower desires? Would he not be altogether the gainer if it could be shown that his soul's probation was to be prolonged beyond the term of his natural life? Might it not then be justifiable for him to take a much less serious view of life, and, without ceasing to be a Christian in thought, extract from life an infinitely greater measure of enjoyment?

Christian thinkers have cause to be on their guard against these supposed dictates of human reason. There is about them the savor of that false kind of philosophy that is the constant product of the mind whose judgments the falling away from God has darkened and perverted.

When we come to an examination of the contention itself, we are at once met by one great and insuperable difficulty. "No single passage can be cited, either from the Old Testament or from the New, which even hints at a continued or second probation after death. Those which may be quoted as bearing on the continued cleansing and perfecting of the elect ... do not speak of them as still on their trial."[21] This is a fact that is admitted by all careful students of this subject who approach it with an open mind, and it is one that any intelligent person may easily verify for himself. The idea, in short, is not contained in the Sacred Scriptures, unless, indeed, it be extracted from an expression here and there, made to yield such a meaning by a strained and artificial interpretation. Such exegetical tricks, however, can scarcely satisfy honest minds. *Fairly* interpreted, all Christ's statements respecting the period of man's probation can have but one meaning, and that points clearly and emphatically in the opposite direction.

And is it conceivable that, if it were otherwise, our Lord would have been silent on the subject, knowing, as He must have known,

[21] Henry Nutcombe Oxenham, *Catholic Eschatology and Universalism: An Essay on the Doctrine of Future Retribution* (London: Basil Montague Pickering, 1876), 123.

the moral difficulties that the doctrine involves and the opposition that it was bound to encounter? Is it at all likely that, rather than disclose such an important truth to us, He should have taken pains to hide it and to deliberately mislead us? It is unreasonable, if not irreverent, even to entertain such a thought and to attempt to reconcile it with all the other utterances so clearly pointing the opposite way. The impossibility of such a compromise becomes apparent as soon as we examine these utterances with the thought of a continued probation after death in the mind.

And can we forget that most solemn parable of Dives and Lazarus, uttered by Christ Himself for the express purpose, it would appear, of warning us "that this present life is the time of trial, and that after death it will be too late to change"?

It is possible, of course, to pervert reason and to empty the simplest human language of its plain and self-evident meaning—some modern rationalizing theologians are expert hands at this kind of work—but do men of common sense and of unperverted judgment discover a way of compromise? Can they reconcile the belief in continued probation after death with the lesson and warning conveyed in this one parable?

And how does the matter really look from the standpoint of fact and human experience? In contemplating the human mind, we have to distinguish, and do distinguish, between two conditions: between a state of development and a state of maturity. A condition of development must, at some time or other, reach its end; it cannot go on indefinitely. In a certain sense, man's education, in the temporal sphere, may perhaps be said to go on indefinitely and to continue during the whole of life; but this is true only in respect of the intellectual side of his nature. He is apt to widen his views, and to change his mind, as he gathers additional experience and knowledge. But it is not so in the moral sphere. There the process of change and improvement is, for the most part, limited to the period of development, and a state of maturity is reached after a time. At a certain age, or after certain moral experiences of life, the character is apt to become definitely fixed, and by it the soul's life in this world is determined. We speak of a man as *having* a strong or a weak character, and our conception is that of a point reached, of a definite moral state and condition attained. Indeed, the intellectual difficulty would seem to lie altogether the other way. We experience it in the effort to conceive of a great moral change taking place after a certain age and condition of development have been reached: *after a man's character is formed.*

And what ultimately determines and shapes character one way or the other is, of course, the mind's attitude toward the supernatural —spiritual principles and interests cultivated or neglected, life and conduct regulated according to God's will and law or according to conventional standards and worldly maxims.

The educational process of earth must necessarily form either a natural man or a spiritual man.

Now admitting, as we must admit, that death is, in any case, some kind of terminus, since the soul's environment is completely changed, what reason have we for supposing that God will bring further and extraordinary influences to bear upon that soul in its separated state?

Scripture, as we have seen, lends no support to any such supposition. The observations of life, on the other hand, point to a tendency to fixedness of character that neither pain, nor mental or moral suffering, nor the agonies of death itself would seem to affect in some instances. The will has resisted the invitation to repentance coming from without; it has resisted the admonitions of conscience coming from within. It has consequently missed the very aim and purpose of life. But what meaning and rationale would there be in life if a reversal of this process could be conceived to be commencing immediately after death? In that case, why was man put through the painful experience of earth life at all? If a probation be possible in the separated state, why was he not born into that state; why did it not commence immediately upon his creation?

But, putting aside for a moment the question of the possibility or impossibility of a change of mind after death, can there be a true test of the will in the separated state?

Could any response of man to external invitation or internal monition be of the same moral value as a response made in the body and amid the earthly environment? A test of will surely can be conceived to exist only where two conflicting attractions exist. But, in the other state, the earthly life and its fascinations will have ceased to be; the bodily senses will no longer be alluring the will; all mundane attractions will have passed away. The spiritual end will be seen to be the only rational end of life and the only end now possible. Can a Godward decision under such conditions be of any moral value? Could it be said to be a free choice of the will? Can it be called a choice at all? Is it not more than probable that any such choice would be reversed could the soul, by any chance, regain possession of its body and suffer the attractions of the old environment?

It is a fact well known to all students of psychic phenomena that spirits claiming to be the unhappy and disappointed souls of the dead seek communication with the living and endeavor to incorporate themselves in some body so that they may relive their old earth life. The objective reality of these communications can no longer be denied. Have we, in some of these phenomena, occurring spontaneously, a confirmation of the truth of the doctrine we are considering? Is the other world itself bearing witness to the truth of Christ's teaching in an age of flippant unbelief and apostasy?

In any case, it will be admitted that there can be no merit and no evidence of goodwill in choosing God where no other attractions exist to draw the soul. An acceptance, on the part of the world-loving soul, of conditions that leave no possible alternative would be of the nature of a forced surrender. It could not be an exercise of free will. And a change of mind, under such circumstances, could neither bring happiness nor produce true spiritual development. All purification is progressive and consists in a resistance to adverse and opposing conditions. It is effected by the constant action of the free will, clearly recognizing and heartily and consistently embracing and cultivating the higher good. But given that man is a composite being, such a process becomes unthinkable in the separated state.

Some people seem to imagine that the act of dying has in it some peculiar sanctifying virtue, but what is there in physical death that should lead us to suppose this? It is but a casting aside of the soul's outer garment, its removal from its earthly environment. Physical death, terminating the temporal state and the season of admitting of a change of mind and disposition, of undoing unkindly deeds and unsaying hard words, is, from the standpoint of our present knowledge, far more likely to end the time of probation than to prolong it. The soul, removed from its earthly tenement, and the natural sphere of its operations, is certainly, so far as we know, no longer in a position to undo the past, even if it would. It has ceased to be in touch with it and its separate events, while their moral results, which have gone to form the character, are permanent and abiding realities.

But, admitting for a moment the possibility of a moral change after death, have we any good ground for supposing that additional light and knowledge are likely to effect it? Do we not already know far more than we practice? The devils "believe and tremble" but are not thereby softened or sanctified (James 2:19). In what imaginable way can truth be so put as to reach the heart that has become hardened?

It is instructive to note that even thoughtful rationalists, while waging war against the orthodox doctrine of Hell and the belief in a future condition of misery, are constrained, by their study of man's psychic nature, to insist upon a state after death that amounts to much the same thing. They fully recognize the law that is at work, and they know that, by the normal operations of that law, a condition of soul is apt to be created that is scarcely likely to be effected by additional influences brought to bear upon it.

In an article on "the Nature of Retribution" that appeared in the *Light of Reason* some time ago, the writer said:

> It is a well-known fact of daily life that the thing we do for the first time with difficulty is done the tenth or the hundredth time with ease, until at last the doing of it is second nature. The nervous system becomes the willing partner of the moral life and, little by little, the chains of an acquired tendency are bound round the victim, and "he that is unrighteous" brings forth fruit after his kind.
>
> This is true of the physical, the mental, and the moral life. The disused limb becomes the atrophied limb; the unused faculty means loss of that faculty; the rein given to the passions today means loss of controlling power tomorrow.
>
> We make the fight harder for ourselves and the conditions harder to grapple with and overcome. As, one by one, the cells of the physical organism die, they are replaced by new ones fashioned in accordance with the tenor of the mind and the habit of the life, so that in our flesh we reap the consequence of our thought. As, one by one, wrong

choices are made, the evil thought or the evil action tends to become less volitional and more automatic, and our nervous system is no longer our servant, but our tyrant. Thus we become bound in the chains of habit, and habit is only another name for character, and character *may* be only another name for retribution.

It is a terrible thought. None of the hells invented by theologic superstition is half so awful as this.

"Let us remember," says a writer already quoted,

> what is one of the tritest truisms in ethics, the essential tendency of habits to become inveterate. Every student of Aristotle will be familiar with the principle, and all experience confirms it. But there is no reason for supposing that the laws of our moral being will be revolutionized in a future state. Granting, therefore, for argument's sake, that the time of probation may be indefinitely prolonged after death, what right have we to assume that "he who is filthy will not be filthy still"? So far as we have any data for judging, the contrary is far more probable.... How can we be sure, to say the very least, that the will, which in this world remained obdurate to the last, will certainly in the next world yield to the gracious influence it had finally rejected here?[22]

Again, it must be clear upon reflection that if, in accordance with a law of God, man's trial time were prolonged indefinitely, additional agencies being constantly brought to bear upon him, it would be within man's power to defy God. He would, in a sense,

[22] Oxenham, *Catholic Eschatology*, 45–46.

be compelling God to endure his sin and to bear with the manifestation of his perverse and rebellious will. Such a law would be putting God at the sinner's mercy. The very knowledge that a return to God is possible whenever he should begin to weary of his deliberate opposition would tend to confirm a hardened nature in that opposition and would fill the spiritual universe with beings whose ultimate destiny would be forever trembling in the balance.

But such a state of being is unthinkable in a universe of order, where, for good or evil, all things created tend, after a period of development, to reach some final and fixed state of existence.

Again, it might be asked: Is it not conceivable that the pain, consequent upon the severity of the judgment after death, will produce the requisite moral change? This, however, is at best a purely gratuitous hypothesis.

Pain in itself has no converting power. Suffering willingly endured has, to be sure, under the gospel dispensation, a salutary, what may be called a kind of sacramental, efficacy, derived from the Passion of Christ. But it works *ex onse operantis* only; its effect depends wholly on the use that is made of it, and it only hardens and brutalizes those whom it fails to sanctify. There is a terrible truth, which experience abundantly bears out, in those inspired words, applicable alike to the state of obstinate sinners in this life and of those who are finally confirmed in their evil will in the next: "And they gnawed their tongues for pain, and blasphemed the God of heaven because of their pains and their sores, and repented not of their deeds" (Rev. 16:10–11).

> A soldier's life is a hard and painful one, but the army is no school of saints. In this life bad men are usually made worse by pain; why should we assume that it will certainly transform them in the next? I am speaking, be it remembered,

> of those who die unconverted, not of the imperfect who die with the germs of faith and repentance, however invisible to human sight, already in their souls, and whose initial conversion is perfected in the "willing agony" of purgatorial chastisement. And I repeat, that there is no ground whatever for assuming that the discipline of pain, which only hardened them on earth, will convert and purify them in the world beyond the grave.[23]

Dr. Farrar, too, fully admitted this. He wrote: "Do not think that repentance is an easy thing; and be quite sure of this, that the longer it is delayed, the less easy does it become, and the more terrible are the consequences, both here and hereafter, which the delay involves."[24]

"In Hell," writes Baron von Hügel, "the deliberate active will is bad from the first and only various partially deliberate wishes and tendencies are good, but cannot be brought to fruition in a full virtuous determination of the dominant character of the soul and hence *this* state has no end."[25]

How frequently is the permanence and fixedness of character demonstrated in the phenomenon of what is termed "deathbed repentance"? A deathbed repentance may, of course, be perfectly sincere and effective, but so far as human judgment can go, it often is not so. All priests and ministers of religion know of instances in which the moral experiences, passed through during a critical illness, and the admissions made are disowned when recovery unexpectedly takes place. How often is the supposed penitent

[23] Oxenham, *Catholic Eschatology*, 47.

[24] Farrar, *Eternal Hope*, 152.

[25] Baron Friedrich von Hügel, *The Mystical Element of Religion*, vol. 2 (London: J. M. Dent, 1908), 227.

positively ashamed of the "weakness" he has shown, and how often he returns to his former attitude and mode of life? The character was too definitely formed to admit of any appreciable change. I know of a case in which the supposed penitent crossed the street to avoid meeting the man to whom he had made a manifestation of conscience when he believed himself to be on his deathbed!

But it is often urged (and this is perhaps one of the most familiar difficulties) that the time allotted to us as the period of our probation is too short; "that the longest and most eventful career does not give full play to the latent capabilities of even a very ordinary character." This difficulty, however, could be maintained only if it could be shown that the time of our lives, given us for our moral regeneration, is too short in proportion to our capabilities and opportunities. And who will presume to judge accurately in such a difficult matter? Who can see as God sees? He who accurately knows our capabilities and who has appointed our time of probation is surely free to decide when it is to terminate for each one of us. And it cannot be denied that, considering the moral stimulus that it involves, it was necessary that God, in His wisdom, should leave us in ignorance as to the exact time of its termination.

Indeed, the plea as to the shortness of time is a subtle and perilous self-deception. There is a certain appearance of reasonableness about it at first sight; but it vanishes when the matter is really carefully looked into and the difficulty analyzed. It is not, let it be borne in mind, a question of certain acts and things done or left undone but of a *character formed*—finally formed perhaps in a moment of time. This moment may come early in life; it may come late. No mortal man can tell when the decisive crisis in the soul's life is reached from God's point of view. "He to whom a thousand years are as one day can, if it so please Him, as infallibly test the entire bent and purpose of the will by a single trial as after a course prolonged through countless ages." If the period of probation is to be limited at all, it matters nothing to the unerring judgment of the All-Wise at what precise point the term is fixed. He alone can know what is in the heart of man. One thought, one decision, one action sometimes sums up the complex moral life extending over a course of years, and, so far as we know, that thought or decision may fix the character. The probability, indeed, from our point of view, is that it does so. And from this standpoint, our time of probation is really much longer than would seem necessary.

In any case, a *change* of mind while still in the body, a turning of the will to God and a resolution to obey His law and to live for Him, presents no difficulties. It is a moral act, an attitude of the soul requiring for its manifestation a mere fraction of time, and, by that fraction of time rightly employed, the soul may secure its escape.

No right-thinking man will be disposed to deny that with the light, the opportunities, and the aids vouchsafed to him, he might at any given moment be a much better man that he really is. Life, broadly speaking, is long enough to enable a man to achieve his aims in the temporal order. It is not too short to enable him to achieve its end or purpose in the spiritual order.

In most instances, it affords the necessary time, opportunity, and means for this purpose. Consider with what intenseness and persistence young and old strive after earthly distinctions and possessions. Think of the energy, the courage, the determination, the restless perseverance with which, day by day, for thirty, forty, or fifty years, men pursue their temporal ideals; how incessantly the one all-absorbing aim occupies the mind; how they trample underfoot all considerations of health and personal well-being—how, to the very last hour of life, the interest of their business or profession occupies their thoughts. Can any sane man presume to say that a life so full of restless enterprise and achievement is too short to develop the powers of the soul, to rightly train and direct the will, and to seek the attainment of that "holiness without which no man shall see the Lord"?

A hundredth part surely of the energy displayed would be sufficient to achieve the all-important end.

But with all the means of grace persistently and consistently neglected, with God and His claims ignored, despised, and forgotten, can man in reason claim forgiveness because of his brief opportunity and compel God to let him achieve his end in spite of his neglect and rebellion? Can the Creator of the world be accused of vindictiveness and cruelty because He will not regulate his actions or modify the operation of His laws according to the caprice and humor of His creature?

It will furthermore be conceded that, with the vast majority of men, the belief in a continued probation after death diminishes the seriousness of life as the one trial time for eternity. It tends to relax our moral energies. "Release from the notion of eternal punishment would be felt by the great mass as a release from the sense of moral obligation; and, relying on the certainty that all would be sure to be right at last, men would run the risk of the intermediate punishment, whatever it might be, and plunge into self-indulgence without hesitation."[26]

It cannot be sufficiently insisted that the fear of punishment plays an infinitely greater part in the evolution of man's moral life than is commonly supposed. We should look upon the actual facts of life and upon man as he really is; we are then scarcely likely to be led astray by high-sounding phrases and by arguments so dear

[26] J. B. Mozley, D.D., *Essays, Historical and Theological*, vol. 2 (London: Rivingtons, 1878), 296, 298.

to the modern mind. The exceptionally clear and uncompromising declarations of Holy Scripture on this subject could not have been uttered without a very definite aim, and it should not be forgotten that He who knew what was in man

> has used language which, on the hypothesis of a probation after death, loses all, or nearly all, its force.
>
> What mean those repeated warnings about the thief in the night; the sudden return of the master of the house, or of the bridegroom; the two men in one bed; the two women at the mill; the two men in the field, of whom one was taken and the other left; what mean those reiterated exhortations of Christ and His Apostle to continual watchfulness but that life is short, the time of death uncertain, and there is no repentance in the grave?[27]

"How much," wrote Mr. Gladstone,

> do we know of the lot of the perversely wicked? They disappear into pain and sorrow; the veil drops upon them in that condition. *Every indication of a further change is withheld,* so that if it be designed it has not been made known, and is nowhere incorporated with the divine teaching. Whatever else pertains to this sad subject is withheld from our too curious and unprofitable gaze. The specific and limited statements supplied to us are, after all, only expressions, in particular form, of immovable and universal laws—on the one hand, of the irrevocable union between suffering and sin; on the other hand, of the perfection of the Most

[27] Rev. H. N. Oxenham, "Eternal Perdition and Universalism, Part II," *Contemporary Review* 27 (December 1875–May 1876): 437.

> High—both of them believed in full, but only in part disclosed, and having elsewhere, it may be, their plenary manifestation in that day of the restitution of all things for which a groaning and travailing Creation yearns.[28]

4. Why Does God Not Destroy the Finally Impenitent Soul?

Punishment, it is urged, may be a moral necessity. The divine law of justice may, in a way we do not understand, demand its infliction. But why should that punishment be unending? Why does not God either allow the rebellious sinner's conscious life to terminate at death, or, after a punishment sufficient to vindicate His moral law, terminate it after death? A persistent refusal to strive after the true end of life when that end has been clearly perceived may conceivably leave no other alternative. The law is there that "without holiness no man shall see the Lord." The very recognition by the sinner, on the other hand, of a happiness that might have been won but that, in spite of a thousand warnings, has been forfeited, might in itself be regarded as such a sufficient punishment.

And some such method of maintaining the moral order of the universe, if not quite in accord with our moral feelings and intuitions, would at least be reconcilable in some degree with our sense of the just proportion of things and with our reason—it would relieve the distressed mind of that dreadful nightmare that is created by the belief in a permanent state of unhappiness.

It is impossible not to sympathize with the thoughts and feelings that have prompted this question. It sounds like the despairing cry

[28] Right Hon. W. E. Gladstone, *Studies Subsidiary to the Works of Bishop Butler* (Oxford: Clarendon Press, 1896), 259.

of a soul finding itself face-to-face with a terrible and unwelcome but nevertheless incontrovertible truth. It is another effort of the human reason to find some way of escape out of an overwhelming difficulty. But there is probably no theory propounded in connection with this subject that rests upon a more unstable and impossible foundation. The annihilation of the wicked at death or "after death is a notion so purely artificial and gratuitous in itself, so directly in the teeth of all scriptural and traditional authority, and so violently opposed to the rudimentary instincts of natural religion, that it is never likely to take root and to spread. It is a mere clumsy attempt to cut the knot of a difficulty which its authors cannot solve by introducing another far more fatal one in its place."[29]

If we have a moral difficulty in conceiving of a God who inflicts infinite punishment upon a soul rebelling against His known laws, what are we to think of a God who first punishes and then destroys?

Hell, after all, might be conceived of as a state of suffering merely from the point of view of a higher state of glory and delight; it might look different from some other point of view. We have here on earth conditions of pain and anguish that cannot be expected to cease during life but that we nevertheless consider infinitely preferable to death and extinction. But the thought of punishment after death followed by the soul's extinction surely involves a moral difficulty that is infinitely greater than that which this theory is propounded to solve.

At all events, it is certain that the idea of annihilation, of the extinction of our conscious personality by death or after death, is a conception contradicted both by Christianity and by our elementary religious instincts. It is *because* their witness to the contrary is so clear and emphatic that the doctrine of Hell and of future

[29] Oxenham, *Catholic Eschatology*, 52–53.

punishment awakens in us such serious thought and engages our interest at all.

The schoolmen argue that the animal soul, being produced by secondary causes at its first creation and thereafter by the process of generation, is mortal and perishable. We read in Genesis: "And God said, *Let the earth bring forth* the living creature after his kind" (1:24, emphasis added).

The spiritual soul of man, on the other hand, was and is produced by the direct creative energy of God and is consequently, by its very nature, immortal and imperishable. "And the LORD God ... breathed into his nostrils the breath of life; and man became a living soul" (Gen. 2:7). The distinction is clear and is expressed in those familiar words of Ecclesiastes: "Then shall the dust return to the earth as it was: and the spirit shall return unto God who gave it" (12:7).

The spirit is immortal by reason of its origin and essential nature, being independent of, and distinct from, any element of a mortal and perishable character.

The materialistic philosophy, as is well known, has done its best to discredit this reasoning by false methods of argument and by mistaken inferences from scientific facts. The most recent psychological research, however, has established the fallacy of that philosophy, and no thinker of note holds it today. Numerous experiments have shown conclusively that while there is a certain interdependence between mind and body, there are manifestations that demonstrate the former's independence of the latter under given conditions and its spiritual qualities and characteristics. A spiritualistic philosophy consequently has taken the place of the materialistic one.

And the universal consciousness of and belief in a future life, of course, confirm the accuracy of the Scholastic reasoning. Nothing else could explain the origin and persistence of that belief in all primitive races that could not possibly have acquired it from contact with Jewish or Christian teaching. Were the notion of the possibility of annihilation at death or after death possible to human nature, the belief in future rewards and punishment could not, in view of man's downward tendencies and sensual cravings, have been preserved. The development of primitive religions, expressing themselves in sacrifice and expiatory rites for the benefit of the living and the dead, would have been impossible, and human evolution would have taken an entirely different direction.

And the mysterious and complex manifestations of the human conscience, too, confirm it. For when we analyze these manifestations, so authoritative and persistent in their nature, we come in the last instance to the innate conviction of the life after death and the responsibilities that it involves.

If the mind were capable of seriously entertaining the conception of annihilation at death, the tortures of a sin-stained conscience, the manifestations of remorse and fear, in callous natures that have never come under religious and educational influences, would be simply incomprehensible. They would be phenomena for which there is positively no place in the universe and for which we could assign no cause. For, even if early training or "inherited tendency" could in some measure be held responsible for such soul experiences, neither could be considered an *adequate* cause since men do constantly and successfully reject or improve upon other educational and moral principles that they have inherited or imbibed.

Other valid arguments demonstrating the spirituality of the human soul might be adduced from the phenomena of consciousness and free will.

All true science, therefore, and accurate thought go to demonstrate the indestructibility of the human spirit and repudiate the notion of its annihilation at death.

It must be clear, moreover, that with the assumption of man's annihilation, consequent upon his rebellion against his Creator and his disobedience to His known laws, anything like order would disappear from the sphere of God's divine government. If it were certain that God would hereafter annihilate the incorrigible sinner and that no punishment, strictly speaking, need be feared, would there not cease to be any distinction between small and great sins as soon as a certain condition of soul had been reached? The sinner, convinced that he has forfeited salvation and that he will be wiped out of existence, would probably continue in sin and rebellion against God and thus triumph over God. Indeed, he might be conceived as rejoicing at his success in having conquered God.

The moral effect, therefore, of such a doctrine would be simply disastrous. It would have anything but a constraining influence upon human life. There are natures who, if they had nothing to fear but future extinction, would go to any length in their career of vice and defiance of moral laws. It is the vague sense of the possibility at least of the truth of the Christian doctrine that keeps them within bounds, supported, as it unquestionably is, by the witness of the individual conscience, however faint and indistinct it may be in some cases.

But, granting for a moment that the words of Christ admit of an interpretation favorable to this theory, how would the matter look from the standpoint of the sinner? In its logical inference, would it not mean his victory over God and the ultimate triumph of sin? Would not God be putting it within the power of man to compel Him to destroy a creature that He has created and constituted for His glory?

In creating man, God surely desires man's being; it is therefore unreasonable to suppose that He can at the same time desire his not being. We can believe that man may, by a sinful life, place himself outside the sphere of God's love and mercy, but we cannot surely suppose that he can, by any act of his own, place himself outside the sphere of God's rule and government and thus evade his eternal destiny. The very thought involves an absurdity and limits the Creator's power over the creature.

And assuming that God, to vindicate His law, inflicted upon the sinner, incapable of union with Him, a proportionate punishment in the present life, would it not still be in the sinner's power to terminate that punishment by suicide, and thus to outwit and defy God?

5. Will Not the Thought of Hell Render Impossible the Happiness of Heaven?

It is contended that if Hell means misery and ruin for the lost, Heaven cannot possibly mean peace and happiness for the saved. Earthly bonds are scarcely likely to be entirely severed by the change that we call death. If our complex and undivided individuality survives that shock, memory, too, is bound to survive it in some form. And, in Heaven, memory will be occupied with the thought of Hell. It will busy itself with the destiny of the lost. Looking, as it is bound to look, at the purely human aspect of the matter, it will awaken feelings of grief and sorrow at the severity of their punishment and the hopelessness of their lot. A husband can thus be conceived to be mourning for his wife, a mother for her children, a friend for his friend. Ordinary human sympathy, indeed, would produce this feeling in any one of us on behalf of the lowest and most degraded of our fellow men. And with this sense of separation, and of hopeless loss, how can there be real and unalloyed happiness in Heaven? Would not memory, like a dark shadow, hover over the soul and destroy anything like a real and deep joy? Under such sad and sorrowful conditions, would not the saintliest soul weary of the very greatest bliss of Heaven?

It cannot be denied that the difficulty that is thus apt to formulate itself is a very real and formidable one. It is experienced by many thoughtful and right-minded persons who fully accept the doctrine of Hell, and at first sight, it would seem to be almost unanswerable.

But in fairly considering this objection, two important considerations have to be borne in mind. The first has already been pointed out and is indeed one that we have constantly to remember in weighing the manifold difficulties surrounding this deeply important subject. Punishment and condemnation are not God's arbitrary act. They are the inevitable sequence of the action of cause and effect, the necessary result of a choice deliberately made and persistently adhered to in full view of the inevitable consequences. They have their foundation in the fundamental laws that govern the moral universe. It is no mere figure of speech to say that each man creates for himself his own Heaven or his own Hell. Both states or conditions have their beginning here and now. Time does not exist with God. Throughout the entire period of his life on earth, from the cradle to the grave, man is steadily gravitating either the one way or the other. When he dies, therefore, his sentence is practically already pronounced. God is not likely to put him within an environment with which he has no affinity and with the conditions of which his moral nature is not in correspondence.

The action of this law may be distinctly traced in this present world, and, on the whole, it can scarcely be said to offend our moral judgment. On the contrary, there is a sense in which we acknowledge its righteousness and in which we apply it ourselves in the affairs of our social and public life. Indeed, it is difficult to conceive how any order in the affairs of life would be possible without it. The criminal is not entrusted with the government of the people or with any high office, even though he may possess all the intellectual gifts and endowments necessary for such a post, and we may know his moral state to be due to early neglect or to some overpowering passion rather than to any distinctly evil disposition. It is no particular written law that excludes him, but he excludes himself. He is out of harmony with that moral sphere that is part of the high office in question. And his occupation of it would be a violation of that law of fitness, which is vaguely perhaps, but still universally, perceived and acknowledged by mankind.

And in this sense, we may certainly be said to recognize the justice and fitness underlying the doctrine of Hell already now. We have our intellectual difficulties, it is true. We rebel against this conception of Hell or the other. We scarcely know how to formulate what we really think. Still, that vague sense of fitness is there. It already now governs our moral being, and it is engraved upon the very fibers of our minds! There is, moreover, accompanying it, that deliberate inward conviction, deeply impressed upon the Christian consciousness, that, though there be the punishment of Hell, yet the Judge of the earth will do right.

There are, of course, those who have played tricks with their consciences, and for whom the conscience is no longer a divine witness, who have honestly ceased to believe in a moral order in the world. There are, on the other hand, those who, by cultivating a certain outward calm, succeed in hiding the disquietude of their troubled and tortured minds both from themselves and from others. The modern world has more ways than one of forgetting, or of getting rid of, an inconvenient truth. Still, the fact remains that thorough believers in Hell are, on the whole, strangely calm and composed in the face of so momentous a truth involving such fearful issues; and to say the least, they view the matter with comparative complacency and unconcern. Is it not because they are morally sure that somehow justice will be found to underlie all and that no punishment will be inflicted upon man that he has not deserved and for which he is not altogether responsible?

In the second place, we have to bear in mind that our faculties are imperfect and limited—that we are under the sway of the senses. We cannot see as God sees. With our finite intellects, we cannot hope to grasp fully a doctrine that is part of divine revelation and that discloses the truths of the supernatural and timeless world and order. We cannot even fully grasp a single fact or ascertained law of science. The real secret underlying it escapes us. How can we expect to understand the secrets of a sphere into which we have not yet entered and with which we are only in a measure in correspondence? It may be essential to our well-being that we should know that there is a Hell; it may not be necessary that we should understand the "how," or be able to fit it in with our present conception of things. It is almost certain that we would not fully understand even if some more explicit communication had been made to us.

Again, it is conceivable that the affections of earth will experience a considerable change when we shall learn to distinguish between divine and human love and when we see things in their right proportions. We love a person here on earth because of that person's character and apparent perfections. But we may be grievously mistaken in respecting that person and may regard as virtue that which, from the divine standpoint, is not virtue at all but self-love and selfishness. A perverted nature may, as we all know, be incited to love even by vice.

We cannot, for instance, conceive of a saint loving those whose inner nature is alienated from God and whose character, however attractive from the human point of view, has no beauty or attractiveness from God's point of view. The saint could not love them any longer, since God loves them no longer. Here on earth, we cannot possibly form an accurate judgment of any character and cannot, therefore, say that this person or the other has reached a condition of soul that renders him no longer worthy of esteem and love. We experience a difficulty in conceiving of a fixed and final state of the soul. We look upon every person as capable of improvement, and here and now, Christianity extends its arms of mercy to the most debased and unworthy of men. It is our duty, therefore, to exercise active love toward every man, even though he may have forfeited all claim to our respect.

But the case will surely be very different in the other world and after the Judgment. Earthly love there will have changed its character and will have become transformed. It will view all things in a wholly different light and from the standpoint of a wider knowledge and a more perfect discernment. And it is surely conceivable that, in the light of that perfect love, the soul's nature will experience such a radical transformation that the attachments and affections of earth will no longer hinder its most perfect peace and its enjoyment of unalloyed happiness.

In any case, it is, and must always be, a question of "adaptation to environment." There is a law of fitness at work, the reasonableness of which all intelligent persons acknowledge and in accordance with which they act. The circumstance that thousands of our fellow men are at this moment languishing in lifelong captivity, shut away from all the joys of life, does not seriously disturb our own happiness. Many a father rejoices that he and the world have gotten rid of his reprobate son. Many a wife has known peace and happiness only since the law permanently separated her from her husband. Both implicitly acknowledge the fitness of a law that has ensured their own happiness, and they do not consider that they are enjoying that happiness unfairly and unjustly. Indeed, since aversion has taken the place of affection, is not separation from the person referred to the very condition of this happiness?

Again, it is difficult for us to conceive of any happiness for the sensual man, the brutal profligate, and the heartless money-grubber amid the joys of Heaven, in the company of the saints and the just. Imagine the man whose every thought has been centered on horse racing, on sensual pleasure, in its manifold forms, who has crushed out of his nature every higher prompting and consideration, suddenly translated into the world of spiritual light, where God is all in all and where sensuous delights have ceased to be! Would he himself be happy in such an environment? Would the happiness of those who have striven hard to secure Heaven be seriously disturbed because of his exclusion from them? Is it not necessarily always a question of the law of fitness and of adaptation to environment? Without holiness, *can* any man see the Lord?

These reflections and considerations may not help us much. But they tend to remind us at least that a law of order is at work in the moral universe and that the difficulty referred to here may find its full and perfect solution in our better recognition of the justice and working of that law. They may help us to see that our difficulty is a purely subjective one that may conceivably vanish when we see things from the standpoint of the other world and are no longer misled by the "false seemings" of the sense world.

6. Why Does God Create Beings Whose Future Misery He Must Be Able to Foresee?

This is perhaps the most weighty of all the objections that can be urged against the doctrine of eternal punishment.

Sin, many are ready to admit, may in some unknown and mysterious way introduce an element into the moral universe that disturbs its harmony and destroys its beauty. From the standpoint of the other world, it may be both just and reasonable that the author of the mischief, having introduced it of his own free will and with full knowledge of the consequences, should be permanently excluded from the sphere of the highest beauty and the purest light. But this does not solve the real difficulty of the matter. The fact remains that, however just and righteous the law that thus permanently punishes the transgressor, the punishment is inflicted, and it is terrible and seemingly cruel in its character. And if the laws of the universe made the infliction of such a punishment a moral necessity, was there a similar moral necessity for calling man into being? Why was he created at all, seeing that the end of his existence, in so many instances, is suffering and anguish? Why does not the Creator, being just and merciful and foreseeing—as, of course, He must be able to foresee—His creature's failure and fall, and consequently his permanent misery, abstain from calling it into conscious life? Why does He cause any man to pass through a probation, the issues of which are already fully known to Him? What, indeed, is the object of imposing a probation at all? Is it not an unnecessary and additional means of inflicting pain and punishment, of awakening hopes that are destined never to be fulfilled and aspirations that are certain to be quenched in eternal misery and despair?

The mind is awed and overwhelmed in contemplating these problems and difficulties, and yet they can scarcely fail to suggest themselves. We know that they do suggest themselves to many very thoughtful and devout minds, and nothing is gained by treating them lightly or by perhaps ignoring them altogether. They have their foundation in the very inmost depths of our moral nature, and it is a relief to face them and to formulate them, even if we cannot answer them to our satisfaction or, in any measure, unveil the mystery that prompts them.

But it will be admitted that the difficulty has thus been stated in its most extreme and severe form, and, in viewing it fairly and fully, one very important consideration has to be borne in mind. It is no mere begging the question to say that, from the constitution of our nature, we cannot possibly expect to be able to solve the ultimate mystery of the universe. Our intellects are finite and limited, and we are distinctly conscious of this limitation. We can thus never hope to understand why man or anything was created, or, indeed, how God comes to exist. We are certain that these things lie beyond our ken. Now, clearly, any attempt to answer the question under consideration in such a way as really to satisfy the intellect involves these other questions as to the central mystery of life and the purposes of creation. We cannot ask one without asking the other. To answer that man was created to glorify God may satisfy our religious feelings, but it cannot, and does not, satisfy the craving for a deeper understanding. For the further question might then, and without irreverence, be asked: In what way is God's glory increased by our existence?

But man does exist and is conscious of his existence without being able to explain it. And God exists, and the normal man is both morally and intellectually convinced of His existence without being able to explain it. And the same intuition that imparts the knowledge that God *is* also imparts the conviction that the origin and mystery of His existence are unfathomable. There is the distinct consciousness that, in this direction, no progress can ever be made in our knowledge and perception—that, in our present state, we shall never penetrate the mystery. It brings us face-to-face with our finiteness, which no increase of wisdom and learning and no deepening of our moral perceptions can remove.

Now, the difficulty formulated at the head of this chapter is surely of this order. To solve it would be to solve the mystery of life and to know as God knows—to become possessed of superhuman faculties. We are not evading the difficulty, therefore, when we acknowledge our helplessness and ignorance in this matter and the conscious limitations of our mental nature. All we can do is reason from the known to the unknown and to discover, if we can, analogies between God's method of action as we know it in this present life and His revealed method of action respecting the life that is to be.

And what is God's method of action in the visible universe?

A large number of mankind are born to a life of suffering and pain, both physical and moral. In innumerable instances, they bring with them into life the seeds of terrible and incurable disease that exclude the very possibility of any kind of real enjoyment. In other instances, physical and mental suffering are incurred later in life through negligence and ignorance or, it may be, in consequence of a deliberate transgression of known laws. Declining health and the discomforts of old age are, in any case, the lot of most men. So far as our judgment goes, the individual is, in very many instances, less responsible for this state of things than what we term "natural laws" and "circumstances." In some instances, there is manifestly no responsibility at all; but the pain and the suffering exist, and, whatever our theories respecting their origin, the Author of life must have foreseen it all, must have known that, in calling man into existence, He exposed him to the possibility of extreme and prolonged suffering. And yet He created man. His foreknowledge respecting a world of anguish and of woe did not prevent His calling that world into being. A moment's reflection brings us face-to-face with the difficulty and the profound mystery that underlies it. There are few of us who have not given expression to our sense of it when confronted by some painful incident in life. We are often utterly unable to reconcile such an incident with our instinctive notions of God's goodness and justice. And yet we continue to believe in that goodness and justice. There is an indescribable something within us that tells us that there is a solution somewhere and that they can be reconciled.

The fact, then, remains that God, although He knew that by creating man He exposed him to the possibility of perpetual suffering, nevertheless created him. But if God's manifest action in the matter of our present state is, in the end, reconcilable with our intuitive belief in His goodness and love, why should it not be equally so in matters pertaining to the future life? If, in passing into conscious existence, terrible risks respecting the present life are incurred by the creature, why not equal or conceivably greater risks respecting the future life? Bearing in mind the unity of nature and of nature's laws, is it not more than probable that the law pertains to both states? The risks incurred may, for all we know, be the necessary adjuncts to the gift of conscious life and of free will.

We do not fully understand now; but it is conceivable that we shall have no difficulty in understanding with widened perceptions, and when we know a little more of the Creator's purpose in the universe. "I can see nothing," writes Prof. Jevons, "to forbid the notion that in a higher state of intelligence much that is now obscure may become clear. We perpetually find ourselves in the position of finite minds attempting problems, and can we be sure that where we see contradiction, an infinite intelligence might not discover perfect logical harmony?"[30]

At any rate, it must be admitted that the moral difficulty involved in the question here formulated is no greater than that

[30] William Stanley Jevons, *Principles of Science: A Treatise on Logic and Scientific Method*, vol. 2 (London: Macmillan, 1874), 468.

which is constantly facing us in the known and undeniable facts of our present life.

And in the sphere of our finite human existence, can we, by our own foreknowledge, always save our fellow creatures from suffering and pain? We too are, in a lower sense, creators of life; it lies within the power of our wills to be instrumental in calling other human beings into existence. We are fully conscious that, with the imparting of life, grave risks and perils are incurred. Our children may be born with healthy bodies and minds and may have every faculty for enjoying life—for a time, at least. But they may also be born with crippled bodies and defective minds, and their course, from the cradle to the grave, may be one long period of anguish. Indeed, in some instances, parents are absolutely certain—they have the positive foreknowledge—that their children will be born with the germs of incurable disease in their bodies and that, in giving them physical life, they expose them to the risks of perpetual bodily or mental suffering. Do they, on that account, abstain from calling those children into being? Does their foreknowledge abrogate that law of necessity that seems to underlie the world of phenomena and of conscious life?

Reflection, therefore, makes us recognize two facts:

1. The difficulty suggested involves a mystery that, by the constitution of our nature, we cannot possibly hope to fathom.
2. God's revealed method of action, in the sphere of the spiritual universe, is in perfect harmony with His known method of action in the sphere of the physical universe.

This, again, may not help us much; but it is clearly as far as we can hope to get in an inquiry of this kind. To show that the laws of revelation, however difficult to understand, are reflected in the laws of nature, which we do understand in a measure, is something gained.

Two very important points deserve our consideration:

1. For all *practical* purposes, the difficulty suggested does not exist. We can be absolutely certain that God's foreknowledge respecting our destiny does not in any way affect or limit His action upon our moral nature. The thought is not contained in the New Testament, and it is contrary to all experience.

Hell and its punishments are constantly declared to be of man's, not of God's, making—the inevitable result of our moral freedom. The Christian revelation does not justify us in conceiving of God as creating a world containing a place of eternal torment for rebellious creatures and of then creating those creatures in order that some of them may inhabit that place of torment; but of creating man with every power and faculty for enjoying perfect happiness both here and hereafter. And it is clearly God's *desire* that all men should be eternally happy. He expressly and repeatedly declares, both in the Old Testament and in the New, that He has no pleasure in the death of a wicked man, that He would infinitely rather see him turn from his wickedness and live, and that there is joy in the presence of the angels of God over a repentant sinner (see, e.g., Ezek. 33:11; Luke 15:7). He has made exceptional and marvelous provision for the effacement of sin and for enabling the most confirmed transgressor to become restored to His favor. He is, by the mouth of His Christ and of His Church, incessantly making the most touching appeals to the hearts of all men to choose the way of life rather than the way of death. He had provided supernatural means that are to aid the soul in gaining the victory over its greatest and most dangerous weaknesses. The doctrine of the Holy Spirit alone implies a constant action on God's part in the sphere of the soul's life. And it cannot be denied that these statements of the New Testament respecting God's continued action are most fully and constantly borne out by the facts of our own personal moral experience.

2. We can, in the second place, be absolutely certain that God's foreknowledge respecting our destiny does not in any way affect or limit our moral freedom.

However great our intellectual difficulty in reconciling the two may be, we can be quite sure that our power of making a free choice remains intact. We *know* that we may, at any given moment, exercise that power, if we will, in any given direction. There are influences at work, no doubt, in determining our choice; there are circumstances and personal inclinations to be reckoned with, a host of subtle forces inclining our will and affecting our judgment, but it is certain that we may, by a powerful effort of the will, act directly contrary to them all and allow a higher motive and impulse to set them aside.

The experiences of life constantly bear witness to the truth of this assertion, which any person may test for himself. We are certain that we can, at any particular moment, deliberately choose a path of life and enter upon a course of action wholly contrary to our former habits of mind and judgment—solely for the purpose of ascertaining the illimitability of our individual moral freedom. We can here safely dismiss all philosophical and abstract reasonings.

Our sense, therefore, of the fact of God's foreknowledge clearly does not decrease our personal responsibility. That responsibility must, of necessity, remain as long as *we know ourselves* to be morally free. But this freedom is a matter of constant experience. We are quite certain that, although God inclines and disposes our wills, He does not coerce them. We are to *desire* our own happiness and to make a supreme effort toward its attainment; we are not to be forced into it. As St. Augustine says: "He who made us without ourselves will not save us without ourselves." And, as another writer adds: "It is difficult to see how He could do so conformably with the laws of the nature He has given us."[31] It must be remembered, then, that while the blessing is from God, the curse is from man himself. The condemned sinner has decided his own destiny. It is not as when the first creative fiat of Almighty Charity was breathed over the stillness of the dead eternities to call light and life and harmony out of chaos. This time, the fiat of eternal death issues from the will not of the Creator but of the creature, who has preferred darkness to light and has deliberately rejected the Love that wooed but failed to win him. Most entirely would I repeat and make my own the words with which a great spiritual writer closes his discussion of the relative numbers of the saved: "As to those who may be lost, I confidently believe that our Heavenly Father threw His arms around each created spirit, and looked it full in the face with bright eyes of love in the darkness of its mortal life, and that of its own deliberate will it would not have Him."[32] Or, as another writer puts it: "If there is one thing that is certain, it is this—that no one will ever be punished with the positive punishment of the life to come who has not, with full knowledge and complete consciousness and full consent, turned his back upon Almighty God."[33]

[31] Oxenham, *Catholic Eschatology*, 145.

[32] Frederick William Faber, *The Creator and the Creature* (Baltimore: Murphy, 1857), 352.

[33] "Everlasting Punishment," 123.

3
The Personality of the Devil

If the doctrine of Hell is indisputably part of the Christian revelation, it is certain that the doctrine of the existence and personality of the devil is no less so. "It is scarcely conceivable that any honest believer in Revelation should question—certainly no disbeliever would doubt—what is, in fact, the teaching of the Bible on this subject, reiterated in a variety of forms, and with unmistakable emphasis, in every book from Genesis to the Apocalypse."[34]

What Christ clearly taught throughout the entire course of His ministry is that an individual malevolent power, hostile to the Creator and to His aims respecting man; capable, under certain conditions, of influencing the human will; and having for his aim the moral ruin of mankind, is engaged in a fierce, persistent, and never-ceasing conflict with the world of which Christ, the Son of God and Redeemer, is Lord and Master. This, in simple language, is the orthodox doctrine of the devil, which has been the belief of the Christian world for centuries and without which the teachings contained in the Sacred Writings are simply unintelligible.

That this doctrine, too, should be assailed and denied in the present day need not cause any astonishment to thoughtful persons. An age that dissolves the personal God into a mere abstraction

[34] Oxenham, *Catholic Eschatology and Universalism*, 137.

and denies the supremacy of the human conscience can scarcely be expected to believe in the personality of the evil one. "Neither truth," as a writer already quoted very forcibly observes, "is compatible with a refusal to recognize the Christian idea of sin."[35] And that idea has to be gotten rid of at any cost.

There can be little doubt that modern liberal theology is chiefly responsible for this attitude of mind. It has invariably shown a remarkable readiness to adapt itself to the downward religious tendencies of the age and to furnish the modern mind with good and apparently sound reasons for getting rid of the less convenient and certainly unpalatable truths of the Christian revelation. And it is apt to do its work in a very subtle and cautious way. The accuracy of the biblical statements respecting the existence and action of a personal evil power is, for the most part, freely admitted, but these statements are interpreted in what is called "the light of modern science" and of our fuller knowledge of ancient religious beliefs and conceptions.

It is urged that belief in a second personal power in the universe, opposing himself to the Supreme Creator and gaining, it would seem, in a thousand instances, a complete victory over Him, involves philosophical difficulties of an insuperable character. It seems so much more probable that the Satan of the New Testament is the creature of man's own imagination—a sort of personification of the principle of evil—and it is much easier to believe that, born in the childhood of the human race, he has fed and nourished himself on man's natural fears and ignorances and that it is on utterly false pretenses that he has attained to his present unreasonable and abnormal dimensions. May we not assume, moreover, that Christ, knowing the force and persistence of inherited religious

[35] Oxenham, *Catholic Eschatology*, 133.

ideas and beliefs and the impossibility of effacing them during the few short years of His ministry, accommodated His teaching to the age in which He lived and the people whom He taught and that, were He to appear in our own age and witness our intellectual expansion, He would give a very different account of the matter?

It is thus that modern liberal theology traces for us the natural history of the devil, from his very cradle through the New Testament days and the "dark ages" of the Christian Church right up to our own time, and is at this present moment busily engaged in digging his grave and in burying him out of sight.

It is interesting to observe how rapidly a destructive process of this kind advances on its course, and with what eagerness the human mind seizes upon any theory, however shallow and inconsistent, that is at all likely to free it from the irksome restraints of an unwelcome and inconvenient truth. The doctrine of Hell and of eternal punishment abolished, it was but natural that the doctrine of the personal devil should follow suit, and after that, who will be foolish enough to believe what Christ said about sin and individual moral responsibility before God?

But, we may rightly ask, will this modern method of explaining away the deeper mystic element in the Christian teaching permanently satisfy really careful and consistent thinkers? Will it suffice to answer those deeper questions that the inexplicable moral phenomena of life are so apt to awaken in the mind? With the removal of the devil from the sphere of Christian thought, will the shadow of the evil one, and of his evil world, also be removed from the pathway of human life?

It is sometimes forgotten that there are truths that the awakened spiritual nature of man discerns quite independently of the dicta of any theologian and that there is a sphere in which even the devil does not leave himself without a witness.

But is it really a fact that the modern intellect, accustomed to the scientific method of thought, experiences an insuperable difficulty in accepting this doctrine and that it has ceased to believe in the existence of the personal devil? Would it not be more correct to say that it is that peculiar *kind* of modern intellect that hastily jumps to conclusions and is not in the habit of thinking very accurately on any subject that experiences this difficulty? Is the skepticism spoken of not due to that false religious liberalism that Cardinal Newman defined as "the exercise of thought upon matters, in which, from the constitution of the human mind, thought cannot be brought to any successful issue, and therefore is out of place."[36]

I find as the result of my examination of this subject that men of really great intellect, who are certainly accustomed to the scientific method of thought but who show that greatness best perhaps in the acknowledgment of its limitations, have no such difficulty. On the contrary, both accurate thought and careful observation lead them to the conclusion that the doctrine of the existence and action of a personal evil agency in the world has a good and reasonable foundation. I will here only quote two such men in support of my statement.

"I presume," wrote Mr. W. E. Gladstone, "that most Christians who watch with any care their own mental and inward experience, are but too well convinced that they have to do with 'principalities and powers, the rulers of the darkness of this world'; that they are beset by *a great personal scheme of evil agency*, under which method and vigilance, employing whatever bad means, or even good, will

[36] John Henry Newman, *Apologia pro Vita Sua* (London: Longmans, Green, Reader, and Dyer, 1876), 288.

serve their purpose, are raised in their work of seduction and ruin to what seems a terrible perfection."[37]

The late Sir James Risdon Bennett, M.D., F.R.S., ex-president of the Royal College of Physicians, wrote:

> It may be admitted that there is not a little in the manifestations of many cases of lunacy that may well give rise to the question whether Satanic agency has not some part therein. Religious men of the most irreproachable character and women of unsullied purity of thought and habit will use language, entertain ideas and manifest conduct altogether opposed to their character in a sane state and which becomes the source of the utmost pain and distress of mind when restored to reason.[38]

Again, must it not be admitted that the difficulty that the doctrine is declared to present to intelligent minds is due to a misrepresentation of it and to its familiar popular coloring rather than to the doctrine itself? Can it be said to be contrary to *right* reason?

Reduced to their simple and fundamental principles, what are the truths that historical Christianity presents for our acceptance and of which the doctrine of the personal devil forms part?

Natural religion (expressed in the manifestations of conscience and moral intuitions) teaches man that the true end of life is a spiritual one. Nothing here on earth wholly satisfies. Reason itself insists that, given the existence of God, the daily eating and drinking and the pursuit of the trivial interests of life cannot possibly be its ultimate aim and purpose. Supernatural religion—i.e.,

[37] Gladstone, *Studies Subsidiary*, 213, emphasis added.

[38] Sir Risdon Bennett, *The Diseases of the Bible* (n.p.: Religious Tract Society, 1891), 82.

Christianity—authoritatively confirms and emphasizes this, but at the same time, it declares that, by reason of man's peculiar constitution and composite nature, the attainment of this supernatural end is necessarily a difficult matter. There are forces and influences at work that are calculated to prevent and hinder this attainment. Failure to attain is therefore, from the very nature of the case, possible.

Some of these hindering forces are *natural.* They have their origin in our present bodily state. They operate in the form of love of ease and of physical delights, of temporal desires and ambitions, of an innate aversion to spiritual exercises such as prayer, self-denial and self-discipline, mortification, and so forth. Some are clearly *beyond nature.* They take the form of terrible temptations, of enticements to things that the better nature abhors but respecting which the mind is misled and the judgment is distorted. For composite beings, such as we are, the present life and state necessarily constitute the sphere in which the conflict between these opposing forces must be carried on and in which some kind of terminus and decisive attitude one way or the other must be reached.

Now, is it really more reasonable to attribute these latter forces, so fierce and persistent in their character, to mechanical causes rather than to an intelligent one? Do they not find their fullest and most adequate explanation in assuming the existence and action of a mind and will in opposition to the supreme good and ever seeking to thwart the purposes of God in creation?

In any case, must it not be admitted that, in most instances, these assaults are cleverly and ingeniously directed, sometimes wholly against our wills, with a certain end in view and in conformity with individual temperament and character and disposition? Are we not sometimes startled by the strangeness and suddenness of the assaults and by the cunning craftiness that they disclose?

We speak with horror of the atrocities of wicked men and of the records of vice and sin that disfigure human history and disgrace human nature. We are willing to admit that human nature is weak and altogether imperfect. But if all these crimes and vices are to be attributed to that human nature, in its constitutional manifestations, without some external agency inciting and stimulating it, what would our verdict have to be? Would we not have to pronounce it as simply horrible and diabolical in its essential tendencies and characteristics?

This is a difficulty that does not seem to present itself to the minds of some of our modern philosophers who certainly do not realize that their lofty dismissal of this fundamental truth leads them into infinitely greater intellectual and moral perplexities than those that they are attempting to solve.

The primitive man never had a doubt about the matter. The modern civilized man would not doubt, if he really thought seriously about it and if he obeyed the dictates of his intuition. He would probably admit the more than probability of an intelligence working behind these manifestations of human nature. But the existence of such an intelligence being a truth of revelation, and belief in revelation being held, in some quarters, to be an unscientific attitude of mind, he doubts and equivocates and finds refuge in a meaningless but fashionable phraseology.

This, it seems to me, is the modern difficulty in a nutshell. There is a scientific ring about it; when it is examined, however, it is found to be utterly unscientific and irrational. Intelligent effects and modes of operation must have an intelligent cause, and since that intelligent cause can be neither God nor the human mind itself, it must be some other mind.

This conclusion, I cannot help thinking, must be the result of any consistent and accurate mode of reasoning, and I, for one, fail to see where the flaw in the argument lies. In the matter of the moral hindrances that oppose themselves to the soul's progress and development, we would surely have to recognize the action of an intelligent mind, and of purpose and direction, had Christianity never made any disclosure on the subject.

In recent years, many ingenious theories have been propounded, seeking, in various ways, to explain and account for the mystery of evil that is seen to be at work in the world and in mankind. But can it be said that any one of them has solved the perplexing problem and has suggested an explanation that is really satisfactory to our reason when it is freely exercised? Must we not admit that, when all is said and done, and when all the facts and circumstances of the case are fairly and fully considered, the Christian explanation remains the most reasonable one of them all?

A very suggestive writer has given expression to this thought in an interesting work entitled *Evil and Evolution*. The book is an attempt to turn the light of modern science on the ancient mystery of evil, and the conclusions arrived at by its author are wholly in favor of the personal devil as he is presented in Sacred Scripture. The writer points out that of the three possible theories respecting the origin of evil, the biblical is the best and only reasonable one. It is the one, we may safely add, most completely in accord with the discoveries of recent psychical science. He says:

> Assume that the Creator had an absolutely perfect scheme, vast and intricate beyond all human thought, beautifully harmonized, delicately poised and adjusted down to its most minute detail, and all for the health and happiness of countless generations of life, and assume that a malignant intelligence brings all the resources of his malignity and intellect to the task of disturbing that nicety of balance and

> adjustment, and in the world around us you have exactly what might be expected....
>
> What I am now trying to show is that we are surrounded by manifestations of evil which there is no possibility of reconciling with any Providential government that is at the same time absolute in wisdom and goodness and almighty in power, and that none of the orthodox solutions of the riddle can be accepted, except the most orthodox of them all, the actual existence of satan.[39]

It is impossible to doubt that these sentiments will be echoed by numbers of really thoughtful but distressed minds, who have found themselves face-to-face with this great problem and who have not been able to escape the dreadful alternative.

Those ardent would-be religious reformers to whom the old-world beliefs are merely reflections of human weakness and ignorance, and who welcome in modern unbelief and misbelief the liberation of reason and intellect, are sometimes strangely illogical and inconsistent in their assumptions and reasonings. They are ready enough to proclaim the untenableness of ideas involving, in their opinion, insuperable intellectual difficulties, but they seem to be quite unconscious of the fact that the difficulties that they are thus introducing are really infinitely greater. They certainly do not follow their flimsy theories to their legitimate and logical conclusion. "In the blindest of optimism," says the same author, "they are preaching a God of goodness and gentleness and love, while the real God, that science seems to be more and more revealing, is that horrid nightmare, the God of evolution, whose

[39] George Francis Millin, *Evil and Evolution: An Attempt to Turn the Light of Modern Science onto the Ancient Mystery of Evil* (London: Macmillan, 1896), 93, 30.

schemes have been drawn in lines of blood and tears, to whom nations are but dust beneath His feet, whose trusty ministers are war and pestilence and famine, whose laws are pitiless as death, and as irresistible as the storm."

And what are we to think of the words of Christ? How are we to reconcile these modern views with the character of Him in whose mouth there was no lie. If the language of man can convey any truth at all, His language surely conveyed the idea that there is a personal devil, that he is our strongest and most dangerous enemy, and that one of our greatest perils lies in our natural disposition to ignore or disbelieve his existence. In any case, if Christ was God, surely He must have known whether there is a devil or not. If He knew there was not, how could He have used language such as He did, seeing that He came not to confirm man's ignorance and misbeliefs but to remove and abolish them and to teach him the truth concerning his soul and his soul's life. Here, too, liberal theology surely entangles us in a hopeless and bewildering maze out of which there is no rational and honorable way of escape.

Really thoughtful men, therefore, will admit with the author already quoted "that ... to eliminate Satan is to make the moral chaos around us more chaotic, the darkness more impenetrable, the great riddle of the universe more hopelessly insoluble. So far from a belief in a devil complicating matters, it is ... the only condition upon which it is possible to believe in a beneficent God."[40]

But the widespread rejection of the doctrine of the personal devil is probably far more due to that modern mania for what is "scientific" and "liberal" in thought than to any inherent intellectual difficulty presented by the doctrine itself. As a matter of fact, numbers of persons do not think very deeply about the subject

[40] Millin, *Evil and Evolution*, 7.

at all but are content to echo and to adopt the ideas and theories that happen to be the accepted and dominant ones for the time being. To the majority of men, it is probably an intense relief to get rid of the devil—and to get rid of him on the authority of their own appointed and authorized teachers. They certainly are not sufficiently interested in the matter to think out and to face the greater intellectual and moral difficulties that that denial involves.

And so far as *the most recent* science is concerned, unorthodox theology can scarcely hope for continued support from that quarter. Science, as all accurately informed persons know, has in recent times performed one of its familiar feats of mental gymnastics and has swung round from a materialistic to a very definitely spiritualistic form of thought. The existence of an unseen spiritual world and of spiritual beings—in some instances of an admittedly evil and malignant character—is practically demonstrated. And the step from this admission to the recognition of a superior mind, directing these evil and hostile forces, is surely not a very big one. I, for one, am profoundly convinced that true psychology will, in the course of time, be found to be an aid to the belief in historical Christianity, in a sense and to a degree that few persons can imagine at the present moment. Indications of the direction in which true scientific thought is traveling today are evident on every hand. Fuller statements on this subject will be found in the concluding chapter of this book.

In his review of Flournoy's *Spiritism and Psychology*,[41] the late Mr. Andrew Lang made the following suggestive statement:

> In my opinion, if Mr. Myers is not at the bottom of it [of the attempt to establish his survival and identity by means

[41] *Morning Post*, November 20, 1911.

> of "cross correspondence"], some one whom our rude forefathers would have called "the devil" is; or, at least, something which is quite as unwelcome to science (i.e., antiquated science).

The familiar question "Why, then, does not God exercise His almighty power and destroy Satan?" is a question that we cannot hope and *cannot be expected* to answer. It touches that fundamental secret of the universe that clearly lies beyond our ken. We might ask the further question: "Why does not God destroy us when we sin? Why does He tolerate evil at all?"

It is conceivable that to destroy it and Satan would be contrary to the fixed laws of the moral universe and would mean the destruction of man's free will, in the inscrutable mystery of which evil originated.

For the same reason, belief in the existence of the devil cannot be said to lay upon us the necessity of accounting for the "how" of his existence. We believe in God without being able, and without ever hoping to be able, in any sense, to fathom the mystery of His being. We believe in Him because we trace His action both in the physical universe and in the hidden world of our inner life. In the same way, there is nothing against reason in acknowledging the existence and action of a personal evil power, even though we are unable scientifically to explain his origin and the "how" of his existence. The scriptural explanation is both a reasonable and a sufficient one, and it is accepted where prejudice and a false method of philosophy have not barred the way.

"How Satan exists," writes a well-known theologian,

> or where at the present time or how his power avails, as we are told it does, to contrive to suggest temptation to the mind of man, and to what extent he is aware of what

> is passing in men's minds, so as to adapt his suggestions to their weakness, we are not told, and do not therefore know. But our not being told *the manner* in which his power is being exercised and brought to bear is no proof of the unreality of that fearful being who is everywhere in the New Testament exhibited as the adversary of God and goodness, whether in the individual or in the development of the human race.[42]

But it is impossible to sum up the argument of this chapter in clearer and more effective language than that employed by the author of *Evil and Evolution*.

> If you admit [he says] the creative power and the beneficence of God, I cannot for the life of me see why you may not admit the possibility of the existence, the power, and the malevolence of a devil, and I maintain that all the probabilities are in favor of the assumption that the maladjustments in the scheme of creation are due to the agency of Satan, and are in no way to be ascribed either to the indifference or the insufficiency, or, worse than all, to the deliberate purpose of the Creator. That there is a conflict between good and evil raging all around us and within us is only too evident.[43]

[42] Rev. Charles Reichel, B. D., quoted in Steward and Tate, *The Unseen Universe*, no. 255.

[43] Millin, *Evil and Evolution*, 64.

4

Manifestations of an Evil Spirit World

It is a very remarkable circumstance that, concurrently with the growth of the modern school of destructive theology, there has arisen a movement of thought that is tending in a very different and, indeed, opposite direction. This movement has now been going on for a considerable number of years; it is counting among its adherents some of the most prominent men in science and in literature, and it is arousing the interest of thoughtful minds in all classes and conditions of society. Its origin is due to the systematic study and observation of certain abnormal psychical phenomena, the occurrence of which orthodox science cannot explain but the reality of which it finds itself compelled to admit.

It is not here the place or the occasion to speak of these phenomena in detail or to describe the conditions under which they occur.[44] It is sufficient to point out that they have been observed by men of prominent scientific standing and of worldwide reputation and that the testimony respecting them is practically unanimous. Indeed, so exceptionally strong is the evidence today that the skeptical attitude of mind can no longer be regarded as a sign of superior intelligence but of being very imperfectly informed. The skeptics are those who are either ignorant of the facts that patient research

[44] See J. Godfrey Raupert, *Modern Spiritism.*

has ascertained or whose judgment is based upon presupposition and a priori reasoning.

"I have never yet known or heard of any inquirer," writes a well-known student of psychical phenomena,[45] "who has followed up the research with honest care and vigor without becoming convinced that things do happen which 'common sense' cannot explain."

The conclusions of informed scientific thought may be summed up in the words of two scientific men of note who have devoted many years of patient study to the subject.

"We see then," writes Dr. J. Venzano,[46] "that for the executions of these manifestations, a fresh personality and a fresh will must have intervened, independent of our own and in manifest opposition to the will of the medium; a will, the genesis of which is unknown to us, and for which, as we do not wish to overstep the limits of admitted scientific possibility, we abandon the search."[47]

"All that I am prepared to assert from my own experience," says Sir W. F. Barrett,[48] "is, that neither hallucination, imposture, malobservation, mis-description, nor any other well-recognized cause can account for the phenomena which I have witnessed, and that the simplest explanation is the spirit-hypothesis."[49]

In other words, the existence of a spirit world and of spirit beings, capable of acting upon our present life and of influencing

[45] J. H. Hill of the Society for Psychical Research.

[46] An Italian physician of note.

[47] Dr. Joseph Venzano, "A Contribution to the Study of Materialisations," *Annals of Psychical Science* 6 (July–December 1907): 180–181.

[48] Professor of Experimental Physics in the Royal College of Science in Ireland.

[49] W. F. Barrett, *On the Threshold of a New World of Thought* (London: Kegan Paul, French, Trübner, 1908), 20.

human thought and character, is an admitted fact. No theory seeking to account for some of the phenomena observed on purely natural grounds can any longer be admitted.

Now, it is quite certain—and indeed, abundant evidence exists for this statement—that any accurate summary of the facts ascertained and of the phenomena observed would have to include the following admission: beings of an evil nature and operating with a manifestly evil intent exist in the spirit world. It has been found wholly impossible to deny or ignore this transparent fact. And it is now admitted by all honest scientific and unscientific inquirers. Indeed, all modern spiritistic literature is full of it. There are few persons today who do not know, or who have not heard of, inquirers who, after a period of great devotion to the cause and of earnest, painstaking investigation, have abandoned it because of the evils and perils that have been found to attend it. There are, at this present moment, numerous families in England who have tales to tell of utter misery and sorrow brought on through the spiritistic séance and through communication with the mysterious agents who are drawn into the sphere of human life by these means. Spiritism, as all accurately informed persons know, is, in our time, working unspeakable mischief and moral evil in a thousand homes, both here and in other countries.

It is utterly useless to deny all this. The evidence is too clear and abundant to be resisted, and *it is increasing day by day*. The evil element, as thousands know, to their cost, has a way of hiding itself at the outset; it is, in some instances, even apt to remain concealed throughout many years of inquiry, but an hour or a moment almost always comes when it discloses itself, either by some subtle and pernicious influence exercised upon the unsuspecting mind or in some more direct and startling and even objective manner.

The champions of spiritism and many psychical researchers who are determined to see in spiritism the dawn of a new and "rational" religion, calculated to efface or at least to modify the historic Christian Creed, have suggested some plausible theories to account for this evil element in these phenomena; but none can or do deny it.

In most instances, these spirits claim to be the surviving souls of deceased human beings. They are familiar with the conditions of our earth life. They understand our language and our modes of thought and expression, and they exhibit many of those characteristics that we are apt to associate with certain deceased personalities. Sometimes they present even the physical forms and features of the dead.

And they are apt to speak in high-flown language of the wonderful life of the spirit spheres and of the progressive development through which they themselves are passing. When they are closely questioned, however, and their statements and doings are systematically scrutinized and examined, they give little evidence of any such progress. There are numerous instances on record in which the same intelligences have communicated through the same medium for a number of years, but their tone and moral character have remained practically unchanged. They are as absurd and frivolous and mischievous as they were when they first gave evidence of their presence. When hard-pressed, they almost always admit that they are utterly unhappy and miserable, and they invariably request that prayers should be offered on their behalf, even though they appear to be quite ignorant as to whether these prayers are likely to avail them or not.

The communications received from these "familiar spirits," although sometimes very lofty in their tone, are not such as we might reasonably expect from beings who are imbued with a sense of the seriousness of life and whose moral condition is one of progressive development. They have all the appearance of emanating from superior but fallen intelligences, who are not in harmony with the Creator's purposes in the universe and whose ultimate aim is to defeat and thwart those purposes.

> The contribution of these entities to religion includes the practical abolition of the Ten Commandments, the introduction of revolting heresies into Christianity, and the propagation of heathenism and atheism. All that we know of disembodied intelligences is that they are intellectually contemptible and that their influence makes for the destruction of religion and morality.[50]

Another evidence of the evil character of these intelligences is their constant attempts at deception and personation. This is probably one of the most familiar and well-known characteristics of the phenomena of modern spiritism and psychical research. It can be traced throughout its entire literature of both past and present times, and no experienced spiritist denies it. The amazing thing is that this peculiar characteristic, too, does not disconcert them but that, on the contrary, they make every effort to ignore it or to explain it away. Many instances of the most heartless and cruel deception of this kind have, in the course of years, become known to the present writer,[51] and if a record were made of such cases, there is not a spiritist in the world who could not, from his own experience, contribute liberally toward it.

[50] Elliot Stock, "Occultism in Psychical Research," quoted in *Light* 25 (January–December 1905): 289.

[51] See J. Godfrey Raupert, *The Dangers of Spiritualism*.

In some instances, deceased relatives are personated in a manner exhibiting so much ingenuity, and such intimate acquaintance with their past history and their mode of thought, that the most careful and cautious inquirer is apt to be deceived. Unhappily, in the majority of cases, the deception is discovered only when it is too late and when unspeakable mischief has already been wrought. Indeed, so well known is this deliberate attempt of the spirits to deceive that a theory has been suggested that seeks to explain the phenomenon by the action of a subconscious faculty of the inquirer's own mind, set to work in some occult and mysterious way. And it is surely highly instructive and suggestive to read what so great an authority as the late Prof. Alfred Russel Wallace thought on this subject. Speaking of the theory of the second self, he says:

> The stupendous difficulty—that, if these phenomena and these tests are to be all attributed to the "second self" of living persons, then that second self is almost always a deceiving and a lying self, however moral and truthful the visible and tangible first self may be—has, so far as I know, never been rationally explained; yet this cumbrous and unintelligible hypothesis finds great favor with those who have always been accustomed to regard the belief in a spirit world as unscientific, unphilosophical and superstitious.[52]

The evil nature and disposition of these strange beings is further evident from the subtle influence that they are apt to exercise upon the minds of inquirers.

It is not too much to say that this influence is almost always demoralizing in its tendency. Its peculiar danger lies in the fact that

[52] From a paper read before the Chicago Psychical Congress in August 1893.

it is so subtle in its operations that it may continue for years, while the victim himself may be quite unconscious of it. In some cases, any suggestion of such an influence being exercised is vehemently denied by the persons concerned, even though the fact may be fully apparent to any outside observer. Numerous instances might be adduced to demonstrate the truth of this assertion.

Sometimes this demoralizing influence is exhibited in a general loss of moral tone and of the sense of moral responsibility, the victim's mind becoming wholly dominated by the thoughts and ideas of the particular intelligence controlling it and obeying its every suggestion and prompting. Sometimes the innate faculty of distinguishing between right and wrong is paralyzed or perverted, and a complete transformation of the temperament and moral character is effected. In other instances, an indescribable weariness of life, prompting to despondency and self-destruction, is the characteristic symptom.

I have had occasion personally to study and observe many cases of this kind.

A well-known student of the psychical movement who devoted much time and thought to this aspect of the subject, wrote as follows:

> Intercourse with the spirits is, in this respect in the moral world, what eating opium is in the physical world. Opium destroys the healthy action of the natural powers, and the attenuated frame and feeble gait soon bear witness to the ruinous effect of the poisonous drug which at first produced such delicious and soothing effects. So it is with spiritualism. At first the eagerness of awakened curiosity, and the sweetness of the forbidden fruit, then a sort of paralysis of the spiritual power, inability to make any advance, disgust

> and depression which the miserable victim seeks in vain to avert by a still closer intercourse with the world of spirits.... One other consequence follows occasionally from this dealing with the spirits, and that is a rush of abominable and wicked imaginations. One authentic instance I have heard of, in which this was happily the means of inducing a young lady to give up the practice of spiritualism. In another case it was not merely evil thoughts that were suggested by the spirits; they led on those who had intercourse with them to evil actions also.[53]

But, as the force of statements emanating from the orthodox religious quarter represented by this author is apt to be diminished by the charge of bigotry and religious prejudice, it may be well to quote what a man of physical science says on the subject:

"Of course," writes Prof. Sir William Barrett,

> it is true now, as then, that these practices are dangerous in proportion as they lead us to surrender our reason, or our will, to the dictates of an invisible and oftentimes masquerading spirit, or as they absorb and engross us to the neglect of our daily duties, or as they tempt us to forsake the sure but arduous pathway of knowledge and of progress for an enticing maze, which lures us round and round.[54]

It is surely impossible to overrate the significance of these weighty words, coming as they do from so eminent an authority, who has been a patient and painstaking student of the subject for a number of years and who views it not from the standpoint of a "narrow

[53] Rev. R. F. Clarke, S.J., "Spiritualism and Its Consequences," *Month* 76 (September–December 1892): 206–207.

[54] *Necromancy and Ancient Magic in Its Relation to Spiritualism.*

dogmatism" but from that of physical science and who, we may fairly suppose, started on his inquiry with no preconceived idea or prejudice on the subject. They will be echoed by all who have an accurate acquaintance with the subject.

It has become the custom of modern thinkers to speak and write contemptuously of the views expressed by the older theologians respecting these phenomena. Belief in the existence and action upon human nature of a demonic world and of beings assuming the forms of the dead has come to be regarded as the sign of a fanatical tone of mind and an out-of-date system of Christian thought. Our higher culture and better scientific knowledge are supposed to have permanently disposed of these old-world beliefs. But few persons are aware how rapidly the best and most recent scientific thought is undermining this "liberal" religious mode of thinking and how thoroughly it is establishing and confirming the accuracy of the old-world belief.

Some of the best scientific students of our day are, on the grounds of observed facts, bearing testimony to the existence of a demonic race of beings and of the possibility of the human personality becoming, temporarily or permanently, obsessed or possessed by them.

In his preface to a work by a foreign savant, Mr. Hereward Carrington, of whom the late Prof. James spoke as one of the best-informed and most levelheaded of psychical students, writes:

> Those who deny the reality of these facts (of cases of delusion, insanity and all the horrors of obsession), those who treat the whole problem as a "joke," regard planchette as a toy, and deny the reality of powers and influences which work unseen, should observe the effects of some of the spiritistic manifestations. They would no longer, I

imagine, scoff at this investigation and be tempted to call all mediums simply frauds, but would be inclined to admit that there is a true "terror of the dark," and that there are "principalities and powers," with which we, in our ignorance, toy, without knowing and realizing the frightful consequences which may result from this tampering with the unseen world.

"For my own part," writes Prof. Barrett,

> it seems not improbable that the bulk, if not the whole, of the physical manifestations witnessed in a spiritualistic seance are the product of *human-like, but not really human*, intelligences—good or bad daimonia they may be—which aggregate round the medium, as a rule drawn from that particular plane of mental and moral development in the unseen which corresponds to the mental and moral plane of the medium, etc.
>
> Moreover, if there is any truth in the view suggested (above) of a possible source of the purely physical manifestations, it seems to me that the Apostle Paul, in the Epistle to the Ephesians, points to a race of spiritual creatures, similar to those I have described, *but of a malignant type*, when he speaks of beings not made of flesh and blood inhabiting the air around us and able injuriously to affect mankind. Good as well as mischievous agencies doubtless exist in the unseen; this, of course, is equally true if the phenomena are due to those who have once lived on the earth. In any case, granting the existence of a spiritual world, it is necessary to be on our guard against the invasion of our will by a lower order of intelligence and morality. The danger lies, in my opinion, not only in the loss of spiritual stamina,

> but in the possible deprivation of that birthright we each are given to cherish, our individuality, our true selfhood; just as, in another way, this may be imperilled by sensuality, opium or alcohol.[55]

An interesting letter on "Demoniac Control" by the late Prof. William James of Harvard University appeared in an issue of the spiritistic journal *Light* of May 1, 1897. In this letter, the professor repeats some remarks that he had made in a lecture on this subject delivered some time before and that had evidently been misunderstood or misreported by the press. "I stood up for it [demoniacal possession]," he says,

> on historic grounds as a definite type of affliction, very widespread in place and time, and characterized by definite symptoms, the chief of which are these: The subject is attacked at intervals for short periods, a few hours at most, and between whiles is perfectly sane and well. During the attack the character, voice, and consciousness are changed, the subject assuming a new name, and speaking of his natural self in the third person. The new name may, in Christian countries, be that of a demon or spirit, elsewhere it may be that of a god, and the action and speech are frequently blasphemous or absurd. When the attack passes off, the subject usually remembers nothing of it. He may manifest during it *a tendency to foretell the future, to reveal facts at a distance, profess to understand foreign languages, sometimes speak them, and prescribe for diseases.* The affection may be developed by the example of others similarly possessed. In

55 Quoted in J. Godfrey Raupert, "Vagaries of Modern Science," *Catholic World* 106 (October 1917–March 1918): 340–341.

> all these respects it resembles the medium-ship which is so common at the present day. If one is genuine, the other is, and they must be tested by the same rule.... I contented myself with rehabilitating "demoniac possession" as a genuine phenomenon instead of the imposture or delusion which at the present day it is popularly supposed to be.[56]

In a more recent report on observed psychical phenomena, reprinted from the Proceedings of the Society for Psychical Research, Prof. James expressed himself still more forcibly on this subject. He wrote as follows:

> The refusal of modern enlightenment to treat possession as a hypothesis to be spoken of as even possible, in spite of the massive human tradition based on concrete experience in its favor has always seemed to me a curious example of the power of fashion in things scientific. That the demon-theory (not necessarily a devil-theory) will have its innings again is to my mind absolutely certain. One has to be "scientific," indeed, to be blind and ignorant enough to suspect no such possibility.

This is surely remarkable and striking testimony, considering the quarter from which it emanates, and it can scarcely fail to awaken thoughtful reflection in the minds of those who have accustomed themselves to treat the matter lightly.

It is well known to persons intimately acquainted with the subject that the influence exercised by these possessing spirits is, in some instances, absolutely diabolical in character. The aim seems

[56] "Professor James on 'Demoniac Control,'" *Light* (January–December 1897): 211.

to be the entire subversion of the moral faculty of the individual affected, and this is brought about by means so subtle and crafty that suspicions are scarcely ever aroused until the moral nature is undermined and the will has lost the power of resisting the promptings of the influence that is dominating it. Several instances of this kind, passing in diabolical cruelty all that the imagination can conceive, have come under my personal observation. In one case, it meant the utter and irretrievable moral ruin and subsequent suicide of the person affected. In others, the effects can still be traced in the victims' shattered health and broken constitution.

The lives of the saints surely furnish us with further striking and abundant evidence of the existence and action of a hostile spirit world.

It is impossible to doubt the reality and objectivity of phenomena such as have, for instance, occurred in the life of the Curé d'Ars.[57] These happenings, which continued for years, were a source of much annoyance to the saintly Curé, who found them to occur whenever he was to be the recipient of some special grace or favor.

And it would seem that every saintly life and every effort after an exceptionally high degree of holiness is apt to evoke these opposing and hostile influences, seeking by every conceivable device to divert the striving soul from the coveted goal, and thus clearly demonstrating the reality of the conflict between good and evil that is going on in the world.

Spiritual writers tell us of the signs or symptoms that attend these invasions, and I have been struck by the agreement that exists in this respect between these writers and those who treat of the matter from the modern spiritistic point of view.

[57] St. Jean-Marie Vianney (1786–1859), parish priest in Ars, France.

Unhappily, we are living in times when any but the right cause is apt to be assigned to these experiences and when, consequently, it is but seldom that the proper means are adopted for the cure of the trouble and the relief of the sufferer.

All spiritual writers admit that among the effects of demonic invasion or aggression must be reckoned:

1. An inability to pray
2. Despair and doubt
3. Passionate cravings
4. Temptations to suicide

Compare this with the description of the symptoms of obsession with which a prominent modern spiritist supplies us:

> Weariness, physical and mental nervousness, sleeplessness, a feeling of being burdened by some invisible weight making the light duties of life seem impossible. All of life's prospects begin to look more and more gloomy. There is an impelling haste in what the sufferer says, and a marked sensitiveness ultimating in great irritability.
>
> Often the atmosphere appears dark and dense, rendering it oppressive to breathe. Common objects sometimes appear to vibrate, causing discordant thoughts. The activity of the will, memory, reason and purpose perceptibly commence to fail in the ratio that this foreign external influence gains ascendency. There exists a state of fear, distress, jealousy, suspicion wherewith the least discordant word or stern look will cause weeping or resentment or anger. Connected with this there is a weakening of the vitality and frequently an abnormal strengthening of the passionate nature.

"All exceptional individual efforts at sanctity," writes a learned theologian, "provoke exceptional demonic activity. The cold and indifferent only are left alone." The probability, therefore, is that the less frequent occurrence of these manifestations in our time is due not, as liberal theologians would have us believe, to our higher culture and more scientific mode of thought but to that forgetfulness of the supernatural and that low tone of the spiritual life that are admitted to be the characteristics of these modern modes of thought. There is, in other words, nothing in the modern man to evoke the activity of the opposing forces.

But these demoniacal manifestations, systematically observed and recorded in recent times, surely tend to throw a strong light upon the phenomena that occurred in our Lord's day and of which we have record in the New Testament. They show conclusively how accurate and trustworthy these records are and how hopelessly modern liberal theology has gone and is going astray in these matters. It is surely a marvelous demonstration of the action of God in the moral universe that that same science that not so very long ago arrogantly denied the preternatural is now led, by the sure method of experimental research, to discover that preternatural and, at least indirectly, to avow its mistakes. It is unfortunately not sufficiently well known that the age of liberal and destructive theology is also the age of scientific spiritism, of the rediscovery of the spirit world and of the existence and action upon us of evil and deceiving spirits.

It is thus that, in this age too, God is not leaving Himself without a witness.

A modern scientific writer who has made a very searching investigation of the New Testament records respecting demoniacal invasion, and who speaks from the standpoint of a medical man, sums up his conclusions in the following serious and weighty words:

> The Incarnation initiated the establishment of the Kingdom of Heaven upon earth. That determined a countermovement among the powers of darkness. *Genuine demonic possession was one of its manifestations.*[58]

But it is impossible to carry the argument further without exceeding the fixed limits of this book.

Sufficient has been said and sufficient testimony has been adduced to show that the position here defended is both a reasonable and a scientific one and that, whatever view some may choose to entertain respecting the Christian doctrine of Hell and of the devil and his angels, some of the best modern thought and an honest interpretation of observed phenomena go to show the entire tenableness of this belief, if they do not actually demonstrate its truth.

And the reflecting mind can scarcely fail to see what an amount of light the full recognition of these truths throws upon the doctrine of the Incarnation and of the work and mission of the Divine Redeemer, who, as we learn from Sacred Scripture, appeared "that he might destroy the works of the devil," and who has "the keys of hell and of death" (1 John 3:8; Rev. 1:18).

[58] William Menzies Alexander, *Demonic Possession in the New Testament: Its Relations Historical, Medical, and Theological* (Edinburgh: T & T Clark, 1902), 249.

Sophia Institute

Sophia Institute is a nonprofit institution that seeks to nurture the spiritual, moral, and cultural life of souls and to spread the gospel of Christ in conformity with the authentic teachings of the Roman Catholic Church.

Sophia Institute Press fulfills this mission by offering translations, reprints, and new publications that afford readers a rich source of the enduring wisdom of mankind.

Sophia Institute also operates the popular online resource CatholicExchange.com. *Catholic Exchange* provides world news from a Catholic perspective as well as daily devotionals and articles that will help readers to grow in holiness and live a life consistent with the teachings of the Church.

In 2013, Sophia Institute launched Sophia Institute for Teachers to renew and rebuild Catholic culture through service to Catholic education. With the goal of nurturing the spiritual, moral, and cultural life of souls, and an abiding respect for the role and work of teachers, we strive to provide materials and programs that are at once enlightening to the mind and ennobling to the heart; faithful and complete, as well as useful and practical.

Sophia Institute gratefully recognizes the Solidarity Association for preserving and encouraging the growth of our apostolate over the course of many years. Without their generous and timely support, this book would not be in your hands.

www.SophiaInstitute.com
www.CatholicExchange.com
www.SophiaInstituteforTeachers.org

Sophia Institute Press® is a registered trademark of Sophia Institute.
Sophia Institute is a tax-exempt institution as defined by the
Internal Revenue Code, Section 501(c)(3). Tax ID 22-2548708.